Prince Jack

Also by Frank Spiering

THE MAN WHO GOT CAPONE

Prince Jack

FRANK SPIERING

Doubleday & Company, Inc., Garden City, New York
1978

ISBN: 0-385-12537-2
Library of Congress Catalog Card Number 77–16950

Introduction

The Third World War did not break out in November 1970, but newspaper headlines in every country could not have been bigger or blacker. WAS JACK THE RIPPER OF ROYAL BLOOD? The question was repeated again and again.

It all began in a journal I edit, *The Criminologist,* a serious and scientific publication, not sold to the public, but to professionals in the police, the law, and the forensic sciences.

That November I published an article intended only to interest my readers as a matter of theoretic history and no more. The article was titled "Jack the Ripper—a solution?" The author was an elderly English surgeon, T. E. A. Stowell, C.B.E., M.D., F.R.C.S., who was introduced to me by a famous author, Colin Wilson.

Stowell was about twenty at the turn of the century and, thus, because of his position, got to know several of the people intimately concerned with the "Jack the Ripper" case.

To go back a bit, I was interested in the Ripper in a purely academic way when I was a youngster, intrigued by a mention to me by Sir Arthur Conan Doyle. Conan Doyle remarked to me that the Ripper was "somewhere in the upper stratum," but he would never enlarge on that statement. I then heard of an Inspector of Police, a man in charge of the Ripper case, who had retired to the elegant seaside resort of Bournemouth. This was in the early 1920s, when I was home on leave from my job as a crime reporter on a newspaper in Shanghai. I went down to Bournemouth and ran immediately into frustration. Though I stayed a week, it was not until my fifth try that I cornered my quarry, ex-Inspector Frederick G. Abberline, working in his front garden. He was not pleased to see me, and refused to answer any questions about the Ripper. But when I said I was returning to Shanghai the following week, and was making notes about the Ripper for a book I might write when I was much older, he relented a little. Finally he answered only one question about the Ripper's identity, and I quote exactly: "I cannot reveal anything except this—*of course* we knew who he was, one of the highest in the land." He then went into his house and slammed the door firmly.

There the matter rested for many years, but from aficionados of the case, that same curious phrase was to recur, "the highest in the land." I was always uneasy about it, and always had a strong suspicion which I never put into words.

When in 1970, Colin Wilson put me in touch with Stowell I was not prepared for the careful research, the quiet authority, and the absolute certainty expressed by him as to the Ripper's identity. Dr. Stowell was a sane and courteous man, neither a bigot nor an alarmist. I suggested he should write an article for me, which he did. And as soon as his article appeared, the journalistic fat was on the fire. Our office telephone rang day and night for over a week. Cables, letters, personal visitors poured in on us. Newspapers, magazines, radio networks, and television companies never let us alone and *The Criminologist* achieved more unwanted publicity in a month than it could have bought for a million dollars.

That is the story, and to *The Criminologist* article I must blame the huge flood of "Ripper" books, films, and such of the past seven years. None of these books or filmed accounts has impressed me very much. But now I am *very* impressed by Frank

Introduction

Spiering. He is a dedicated writer, a man who puts authenticated research above anything else. He has probed into the Ripper case, probed with a mind unimpressed by baseless facts, and while I fear he is going to revive the whole violent controversy he, will do so unintentionally. This book is an important one and, I suggest, the last word on Jack the Ripper.

Nigel Morland

Sussex, England
13 March 1978

Foreword

On an autumn afternoon in 1960, two men met for lunch at the Athenaeum Club in London. The younger of the two, author Colin Wilson, had just published a series of articles in the London *Evening Standard* entitled "My Search for Jack the Ripper."* The other man, the one who had requested that they meet for lunch, was a physician in his late seventies, a specialist in brain disease on the staff of St. Thomas's Hospital. He introduced himself to Wilson as Dr. Thomas Stowell. He then explained once again, as he had already stated in his letter, that from the tone of the articles in the *Evening Standard,* it seemed obvious to him that Wilson knew the identity of Jack the Ripper.

Much to Dr. Stowell's apparent surprise, Colin Wilson admitted that he did not know. The identity of Jack the Ripper was a mystery; no one knew his true identity, did they? Yet Wilson later admitted: "As a child I often thought that if some fairy offered

---

* Wilson, who had been interested in the Ripper all his life, later admitted that the articles had been intended to draw attention to his new novel, *Ritual in the Dark.*

me three wishes, the first thing I would ask would be the identity of Jack the Ripper; the thought that it might remain a mystery forever was intolerable."

As they ate lunch, the good fairy, in the form of Dr. Thomas Stowell, related to Wilson that he had known who the Ripper was for the past fifty years.

Wilson was somewhat taken aback. He had heard various theories as to the Ripper's identity, but none of them made much sense. One memory, however, stuck in his mind. A lady in Ascot had told him that her father ran the mental home in which the Ripper died. But unfortunately Wilson had never learned the lady's address and was unable to track down the information.

Wilson listened intently as Dr. Stowell explained that at St. Thomas's Hospital in London he had been a student of Dr. Theodore Dyke Acland's. Acland had been married to Lady Caroline Acland, the daughter of Sir William Gull.† He had become close friends with the Aclands, and in the 1930s Lady Caroline had shown him her father's private papers. The notes related in detail how Gull had treated the Ripper for syphilis of the brain. They also revealed his identity.

Stowell then went on to trace certain elements of the Ripper's life, but as Wilson recalled, "To be honest, Dr. Stowell's method of narration was somewhat involved, and he also assumed I knew a great deal more than I did about the royal family. So I am not absolutely clear about many details in his story, although he later repeated most of it over the telephone, while I took notes."

Dr. Stowell had not sworn him to secrecy, so Colin Wilson, at various times, privately confided what he had been told to fellow authors Dan Farson, Donald McCormick, and Nigel Morland. As none of them dared publish the story, it remained a secret between them for the next ten years.

Finally, when Nigel Morland launched his magazine, *The Crim-*

† Sir William Gull was Physician in Ordinary to Queen Victoria and Edward, Prince of Wales. One of the great medical pioneers in the use of static electricity to treat nervous diseases, when he died in 1890 he left a fortune of £344,000—up until that time, almost unprecedented in the history of medicine. In addition, Gull had been seen on at least one occasion in the East London slums on the night of a Ripper murder.

inologist, he asked Dr. Stowell to write a guarded version of his discovery. "Jack the Ripper—a solution?" appeared in the December 1970 issue of *The Criminologist* and exploded on the front pages of two thousand newspapers across the world:

> LONDON, Nov. 1, 1970 (AP)—The Sunday Times expressed belief today that Jack the Ripper, infamous London murderer of nearly 100 years ago, was Edward, Duke of Clarence, grandson of Queen Victoria and older brother of George V. The Times was commenting on the statement of an eminent British surgeon who said that the Ripper "was the heir to power and wealth." The surgeon, Thomas E. A. Stowell, while claiming to know who the criminal was, refused to identify him in an article to be published tomorrow in The Criminologist, a magazine devoted to forensic medicine and criminology. The Ripper, who murdered at least five prostitutes in London's sleazy East End in 1888, never was captured. Four of his victims were murdered and disembowelled in one of the most gruesome and bizarre series of crimes in British history. The Sunday Times, in commenting on Dr. Stowell's article, said there was one name that fitted his evidence. It said: "It is a sensational name: Edward, Duke of Clarence, grandson of Queen Victoria, brother of George V, and heir to the throne of England. All the points of Dr. Stowell's odd story fit this man."

The following day Dr. Stowell was interviewed on BBC television by Kenneth Alsop. In his article for *The Criminologist* he had referred to the Duke of Clarence as "S." Although he did not stop Alsop from openly identifying the Ripper as Clarence, Stowell did not allude to him by name.

Pressure was now put on Scotland Yard for an explanation. Finally, a Scotland Yard spokesman admitted, "It happened rather a long time ago. We just don't know." From Buckingham Palace, the Royal Family reacted with a firm "No comment." This was followed by their more extended explanation in *The Times* Diary: "The idea that Edward VII's eldest son, heir to the throne, should have bestially murdered five or six women of "unfortunate" class in the East End is regarded as too ridiculous for comment." But of course they had "commented." They were doing everything in their power to discredit Dr. Stowell's story. A day

11

later another attempt was made to refute his revelation. A loyalist staff member at Buckingham Palace had apparently "discovered" a court circular which proved beyond a shadow of a doubt that the Duke of Clarence had been at Sandringham celebrating his father's birthday on the afternoon following the Ripper murder of November 10, 1888.

Meanwhile, Stowell, now well into his eighties, was under a great deal of political pressure. The force of this pressure finally was more than he could endure. A letter bearing his name suddenly appeared in *The Times* on November 7:

> Sir,
> I have at no time associated His Royal Highness, the late Duke of Clarence, with the Whitechapel murderer or suggested the murderer was of Royal blood.
>
> Yours faithfully, a loyalist and a Royalist,
THOMAS E. A. STOWELL

It was the letter of a frightened man. It refuted all that he had previously related. Someone very powerful had got to him and had either persuaded him to write it or had written it for him.

Information was then released that Dr. Stowell had dropped dead on November 8, 1970. At this point, there occurred an insidious series of events. In conjunction with the news of his father's death, Dr. Stowell's son immediately announced that he had burned all his father's papers. Pressed for an explanation, the son, Dr. T. Eldon Stowell, commented: "I have read just sufficient to make certain that there was nothing of importance. The family decided that this was the right thing to do. I am not prepared to discuss my grounds for doing so."

I was intrigued by Dr. Stowell's theory when I first read about it in 1970. In addition to the story relayed by the Associated Press and UPI, the New York *Times* featured more details in its Sunday section in an article entitled "Who Was Jack the Ripper?" *Life* magazine followed with a four-page spread which commented, regarding the Duke of Clarence, "Stowell's tale strongly suggests that high officers at Scotland Yard and members of the Royal Family—as well, of course, as Sir William Gull—were aware he was the Ripper . . . the suggestion is so strong, in fact, that one familiar with the Ripper legend can hardly refrain from imagining the meeting at which it was decided that England must act in the young man's best interests; a meeting held, of course, in one of those splendidly cozy offices—all Oriental rug, cheerful fireplace, polished mahogany and view of the Thames—which Britain's knighted coppers were privileged to occupy at Scotland Yard. Sir William Gull must certainly have attended. One can hear him discussing his patient's 'unfortunate eccentricity'—a malaise lucky, nevertheless, in that it drove him, um, 'to molest only women of the unfortunate class.' One must certainly assume the presence of some powerful emissary from the Palace, sternly forbidding any possible embarrassment to the Crown."

The articles ended abruptly, however, after the younger Stowell's burning of his father's evidence.

At this point, I began to investigate Dr. Stowell's story in depth. It seemed that both he and his theory had been silenced too quickly. Perhaps there actually were forces at work desiring that the full truth should never be known.

It seemed essential that I interview Dr. Stowell's son, although members of the press had tried to do so and had failed in their efforts. I wrote to Nigel Morland, the editor of *The Criminologist*, which had published Dr. Stowell's article. He replied:

> Naturally I shall be happy to help if I can, but Stowell's son is out. When the great controversy started and the old man died, the son instantly burned all the precious "Ripper" files and refuses to answer any letters or queries about his father, the "Ripper" and, indeed, anything!

I met with Nigel Morland, who told me that he had first learned of the Ripper's true identity in the 1920s from famed British reporter Edgar Wallace. However, Wallace had told him that no London newspaper would dare publish the story. In the sixties, when Colin Wilson had brought Dr. Stowell to his attention, Morland recalled that Wilson firmly believed Stowell's story. It bothered him when later, after the controversy started, Wilson weakened in his conviction and eventually backed down completely.

Dr. Stowell was completely genuine, in Morland's estimation, and his conclusions were solidly based.

Moreland agreed, however, that somebody got to Stowell. A tremendous pressure was applied upon him, causing his death.

With Nigel Morland's help, I was able to locate Stowell's son's address: a surgery located on Bath Road in Bitterne, near Southampton. Realizing that the younger Stowell would refuse my request for an appointment, I went there. Posing as a patient, I finally got in to see him.

I found Stowell to be a pale, distinguished-looking man in his fifties. His icy blue eyes stared at me fixedly as I began questioning him about his father. At first he did not seem hostile, only reserved and ready.

> "My father was not the only one—*several people now in their nineties know who the killer was*," he explained.
> "Do you know what was in the file?"
> "I never discussed the file with him."
> "Why did you burn the file?"
> "I am not prepared to tell you."
> "Was it because of embarrassment?"
> "I am not prepared to tell you," he repeated.
> "Were you ordered to burn it?"
> "There was no outside pressure at all." But I noticed that his hand trembled a little as he said it.
> "The sudden complete turnabout from what he said in his article—and the terms he used—'Loyalist' and 'Royalist' leads one to suspect that there might have been—"
> "I am not prepared to tell you," Stowell repeated again.

My feeling in leaving Stowell's office was one of tension and dismay. I felt, perhaps justifiably, that I should keep looking over my shoulder as I boarded the train at Southampton station back to London.

What follows is intended to uncover what I feel to be one of the most frightening political ruses ever concocted to deceive a national citizenry. For almost ninety years, the British establishment's fear of the truth being known has led Prime Ministers, members of Royalty, and Scotland Yard officials to conspire in hiding the identity of the world's most infamous mass murderer.

At times the story which I unraveled filled me with extreme trepidation. I knew that it cost Dr. Stowell his life and at each step in my inquiry I felt as if I too might be threatened.

Much of what follows has either been documented or came to me by way of people I interviewed at Scotland Yard, staff members at Buckingham Palace, in addition to those persons I promised I would not identify—in exchange for information they gave me. I was extremely fortunate in locating a copy of Dr. William Gull's notes, bound in an ancient portfolio, kept in, of all places, The New York Academy of Medicine. The stories of the murders were taken from contemporary newspaper accounts of witnesses' statements at the various inquests, although the official reports of these hearings have been misplaced or destroyed by Scotland Yard. Descriptions of the murderer himself—detailing his physical appearance—are actually taken from Metropolitan Police files. But this book is mainly a reconstruction of what *I* feel did happen, based on everything I read, officially and unofficially.

The most astounding revelation to me was not the identity of Jack the Ripper, but the realization that "the Court" (composed of the aristocracy and various members of government), in exchange for their agreement to secrecy, have used their knowledge of the Ripper's identity to blackmail the Royal Family.

The power of England's rulers ended with Victoria. But more pertinently, it ended *because* of her grandson.

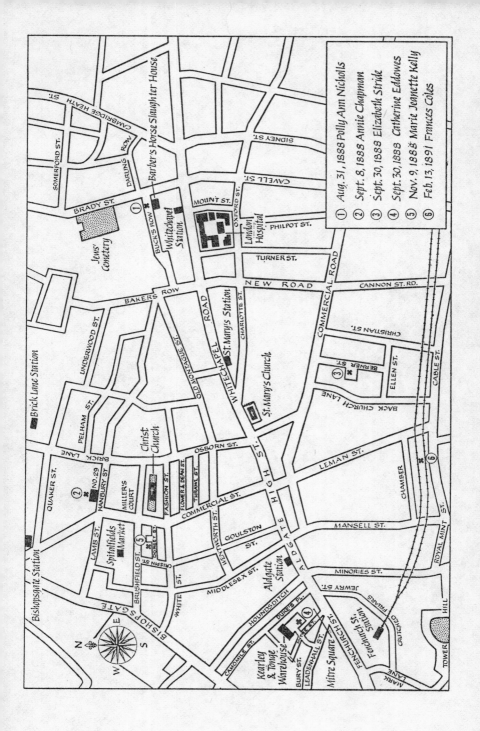

Prince Jack

Chapter 1

THE KNIFE

Albert Victor, the grandson of Queen Victoria, strayed from the company of his homosexual companions shortly after midnight on the morning of August 31, 1888. "Eddy," as his friends called him, was barely missed. The University Settlements were still too packed with the youth of the East End, the regular prey of an aristocratic crowd of "queers" who prowled there nightly. Several of the prettier, more sensitive young boys from the neighborhood had jobs in the posh Marlborough Club, to which Eddy's father belonged. Their appeal was the lack of involvement one feels for a member of the lower class.

As Eddy wandered along High Street through the heart of East London, he passed by the outskirts of Spitalfields. From the herds of humans crowded like animals into courts and alleys, a revolting stench arose. This, mingled with the odor from the piles of rags, rubbish, and the miasma of liquid sewage that permeated the cellars of dwellings stretching across the half mile from Commercial Street to Bethnal Green Road, made the atmosphere almost unbearable. Its center was Christ Church, Spitalfields, constructed in

1729 by Sir Nicholas Hawksmoor, a pupil of Wren's. Throughout the 1700s the parish was occupied by prosperous Huguenot silk weavers who eventually moved westward toward the heart of the city, leaving Spitalfields to a more classless element immigrating from eastern Europe. The industrial revolution propelled the neighborhood even more drastically into decay and, in 1861, when Henry Mayhew visited it, he found "800 thieves, vagabonds, beggars and prostitutes" living within an area of 400 square yards. Mayhew described it as "one of the most notorious rookeries for infamous characters in the metropolis." It was for obvious dramatic effect that Dickens made Fagin cross Spitalfields to reach Bill Sikes in nearby Bethnal Green.

Eddy's father, the Prince of Wales, had once explored the area, disguised in workman's clothes. He had been accompanied by Lord Carrington and Dr. Buchanan, Chief Medical Officer of Health in the Local Government Board. The Prince of Wales was horrified by what he saw. He wandered from alley to alley and finally entered an unfurnished room where a pale shivering woman lay on a heap of rags with three naked children, too cold and too starved to utter a word. The Prince pulled a fistful of gold from his pocket but quickly shoved it back when Carrington warned that the news would spread like wildfire. They might all be torn to pieces by the other inhabitants of the alley, driven crazy by the sight of so much wealth. Lord Carrington later noted that the Prince "visited some very bad places . . . but we got him back safe and sound to Marlborough House in time for luncheon."

Four days later the Prince of Wales delivered a speech to the House of Lords, describing vividly what he had witnessed and urging the Government to take drastic action to improve the living conditions in East London. He himself would head a commission that would sit twice a week for three hours to study the problem and propose what could be done. It was described later as "the only speech of substance which he ever made as a member of the House of Lords." Unfortunately he was quickly distracted by the sudden death of his brother, Prince Leopold, Duke of Albany, in the south of France. From there he had to hurry to Darmstadt to attend the wedding of his niece Princess Victoria of Hesse to his friend Prince Louis of Battenberg. Two months later he wrote to Lord Carrington, "I deeply regret being away from the Commission, and am completely losing the thread of the inquiry; but I fear it cannot be helped."

On his return to London, the Prince of Wales made a grand gesture. He invited radical working-class M.P. Henry Broadhurst to spend a weekend at Sandringham. Broadhurst, upon his arrival, was not allowed to dine with the royal family but was served in his own room each night. He later commented that this was done "in order to meet the difficulties in the order of dress." However, both he and the Prince of Wales apparently had several frank discussions about the problems of the lower classes and Broadhurst happily noted that he "left Sandringham with a feeling of one who had spent a weekend with an old chum of his rank in society . . ."

It had always been fashionable for the British aristocracy periodically to visit "the stews," under the auspices of performing charitable acts, but little of benefit was ever accomplished. Harsh Victorian morality would not permit them to become involved in actually helping the creatures they observed. The Reverend Samuel Barnett, Vicar of Christ Church, argued that indiscriminant charity was one of the curses of London. He insisted that the poor starved "because of the alms they receive."

In Whitechapel alone, four thousand homes had been condemned as uninhabitable. The Artisans Dwelling Act passed in 1875, instead of penalizing slum landlords, left them better off than before. Profits became so great that there was a rash of speculation in slum property. The inhabitants were soon crammed on top of each other and even higher rents were charged.

Finally, philanthropist Octavia Hill came up with the notion of buying the crumbling dwellings in order to find ways to make them yield a steady five per cent return. Tenants were evicted if they did not pay promptly. The theory was that ruthless methods would force the residents to practice principles of thrift. Unfortunately it did not allow for periods when men would be laid off because of seasonal lack of work or periodic recessions. She also did not recognize, or want to recognize, that diseases were rampant in the filthy, deteriorating buildings which she owned.

Because of overcrowding, incest was unavoidable. Lord Salisbury told the story of a friend who was passing through a slum court when he saw two children of not more than eleven years old engaged in sexual intercourse. He ran and seized the lad, who stared back at him in wonder. "Why do you take hold of me," the boy exclaimed, "everybody does it down here!"

Spitalfields was the most squalid area of all. From this quarter-mile hell of outcasts covered with vermin and loathsome skin diseases there was no escape. Sociologist Charles Booth, drawing up his famous Poverty Maps of London, ringed the area in heavy black ink to denote it as "very poor, lowest class . . . vicious, semi-criminal." Its inhabitants slept on staircases, and even in dustbins and lavatories for warmth. Derelict "Jack drinkers," who lived on methylated spirits sold to them in penny jars, slept along the park benches encircling Christ Church. "They are covered with vermin," a Police Superintendent complained to one of Charles Booth's social surveyors, "the police don't like touching them."

Andrew Mearns in *The Bitter Cry of Outcast London*, published in 1883, described one dwelling of families:

> Here are seven people living in one underground kitchen, and a little dead child lying in the same room. Elsewhere is a poor widow, her three children, and a child who had been dead thirteen days. Her husband, who was a cabman, had shortly before committed suicide. Here lives a widow and her six children, two of whom are ill with scarlet fever. In another, nine brothers and sisters, from 29 years of age downwards, live, eat and sleep together. Here is a mother who turns her children into the street in the early evening because she lets her room for immoral purposes until long after midnight, when the poor little wretches creep back again if they have not found some miserable shelter elsewhere.

It was estimated that over half of the children born in Spitalfields died before reaching the age of five.

Meanwhile, prostitutes numbering in the thousands roamed

Thrawl Street, Fashion Street, Dorset Street, Flower-and-Dean, and Commercial Road. Most were chronic alcoholics who, when they had the price of a doss, lived in fourpenny lodging houses. Otherwise, they slept with other down-and-outers in parks or along the railings of Christ Church, forgotten, uncared-for creatures. It was an odd Victorian sentiment that young girls became prostitutes because they were once betrayed by wealthy seducers. If nothing else, the morning of August 31, 1888, would alter that misconception.

Because of the cool night Eddy was dressed in a dark blue serge coat. Its padded shoulders did little to conceal his narrow effeminate body. With his small moustache turned up slightly at the ends, his thin pale face, large dove-like eyes, and his wavy hair hidden beneath a cloth cap with a peak, he was hardly recognizable as a British prince. Dissipation had made him look much older than his twenty-five years.

It seemed inconceivable that an heir to the throne of England should share anything in common with the poor wretches who inhabited the alleys of East London. Yet he too was an outcast. His parents hated the sight of him. His father had long been ashamed of the boy who had caused him so much regret. Eddy had always been an embarrassment.

At his birth he had been shuttled from an icy pond near Frogmore where the Princess of Wales had been watching her husband play ice hockey. No preparations had been made for his coming, yet fortunately a doctor was located in the town. Even his grandmother the Queen had been startled by the fact that there had been "no clothes for the poor little boy, who was just wrapped in cotton wool." The baby, who was two months premature, weighed only three and three-quarter pounds. In the absence of the Home Secretary, Lord Granville, the Lord Chamberlain, who was present as a guest, signed for the legality of the birth.

A sudden pall fell on the occasion a day later when Princess Alexandra learned from the lips of six-year-old Princess Beatrix, Queen Victoria's youngest daughter, that the baby was to be named "Albert Victor Christian Edward, *that's what Mama's decided to call him.*" Princess Alexandra was angered that her first-born son should have been named without her even having been consulted. Victoria, however, was adamant. She demanded that the baby should be christened Albert Victor (the male conjunction of Albert and Victoria) and that all his descendants should bear the name Albert or Victoria until the end of time.

The struggle for power between Princess Alexandra and her mother-in-law, the Queen, quickly worsened. Alexandra was nineteen, a bride for only ten months, yet she prodded her husband to protect her rights. "I felt rather annoyed," the Prince of Wales wrote to the Queen, ". . . that you had settled what our little boy was to be called before I had spoken to you about it." Victoria countered with a vague apology for having "overlooked" a consultation with the parents in naming the Heir, but insisted that it was a national, or to be more precise, a dynastic affair, rather than a personal one.

When she attended the baby's christening a month later, Queen Victoria wore mourning clothes, out of respect for her dear departed Albert, and afterward complained to her daughter Victoria, the Crown Princess of Prussia, that "the poor baby roared all through the ceremony, which none of you did." She further commented that "Alix [her nickname for Princess Alexandra] looked very ill, thin, and unhappy; she is sadly gone off."

After the birth of a second son, Prince George, a year later, Victoria's enmity toward Alexandra increased. Meanwhile the Prince of Wales spent more and more time away from home with various female companions, leaving his lonely, desperate wife to cope on her own. By the time Eddy was eight, Victoria found that Alexandra's methods of caring for her two sons had made them "as wild as hawks . . . they are such ill-bred, ill-trained children that I can't fancy them at all."

Alexandra, herself, had grown increasingly deaf so that she could not hear their howls as they ran up and down through the halls of Sandringham and Marlborough House screaming like banshees. She retreated more and more into a private vacuum, associating with only those few friends whose voices she could plainly hear. Her lack of communication with her children seriously affected Eddy, who grew up with a father and mother

26

now virtually inaccessible. Finally he too withdrew into a lonely fantasy world of his own. He had few friends and fewer interests.

When he was fifteen, Eddy's tutor, Reverend Dalton, wrote to the Prince of Wales about "the abnormally dormant condition" of Eddy's mind which deprived him of power "to fix his attention to any given subject for more than a few minutes." He went on to describe Eddy as sitting listless and vacant . . . the weakness of brain, the feebleness and lack of power to grasp anything put before him . . . it is a fault of nature." Because of Reverend Dalton's comments, Eddy's father, fearing social embarrassment, refused to send the boy to a public school.

The Prince of Wales's greatest fear was of weakness of any kind. It had been drummed into him as a child by his own father, Prince Albert, that a future King should symbolize authority and perfection. Consequently, Eddy's father had rarely been allowed to play with other children and Victoria constantly restricted his activities. His greatest passion became hunting. When Eddy was thirteen, his father had written to him from a safari in India, "I have had great tiger shooting. The day before yesterday I killed six and some were very savage. Two were man-eaters. Today I killed a tigress and she had a little cub with her." The only letters Eddy ever received from his father were about hunting. At Sandringham his father indulged his passion for killing for days, personally increasing the number of game killed from seven or eight hundred to over thirty thousand. This fact was always a source of pride to the Prince of Wales and he boasted of it constantly to his guests.

At Sandringham, the shooting became extremely organized. With the introduction of breechloaders and the new practice of hiring a small army of beaters, the sport was transformed into a military operation. Tenant farmers were expected to sacrifice their crops in order to rear and feed as much game as possible. If they cheerfully agreed, they enjoyed warm relations with the Prince of Wales, and could rely upon his generous help in sickness or old age. If not, they were evicted.

To Eddy it had always seemed absurd that a grown man would waste his time shooting at rabbits and birds. Eddy despised sports of any kind, although he had always enjoyed playing cards with James.

James Stephen was his first lover. They had met at Cambridge and from the first James had dominated Eddy's life. James was jealous of anyone who came near him. It was James who had expressed Eddy's own true feelings in the ironic quatrain:

> *When inoffensive people plant*
> *A dagger in your breast,*
> *Your good is what they really want:*
> *They do it for the best.*

Eddy knew that soon his parents would be looking for a wife for him to marry. Perhaps some German princess or a Scandinavian like his mother. He shuddered at the thought of being carted off and forced to propose to someone he did not know. And then the idea of having to breed suitable, sweet-smelling royal children. It would have been so much easier if they let him choose his own mate. He would have chosen James.

As Eddy continued to wander east along Whitechapel Road, he came to Buck's Row. Hearing sounds in the distance and seeing a building midway down the block ominously illuminated from within by tiers of gaslight, he approached it. It was Barber's Horse Slaughter House, avoided by the neighborhood's residents like an evil omen foreboding human sacrifice. Throughout all hours of the day and night the air surrounding it was filled with the smell and sounds of dying animals.

It was the wail of the horses being slaughtered that struck Eddy first. Then the sight of carts filled with dying animals standing alongside the building. For a second, he almost vomited, but he looked inside the blazing light-filled building.

It was crowded with butchers. Their knives flashed before him and with each slash there was a scream, but not a human scream, as the blood poured forth from the throat of a stallion, then a mare. More horses were brought in from other areas and the ritual continued—as the men in their blood-soaked leather aprons slashed away.

Eddy felt hypnotized. Yet horrified. He had seen deer killed by gunfire and then dressed in a field, but organized slaughter was intoxicating.

Unnoticed, he stood there for a long time, feeling suddenly all alone, cold, trembling inside. For the first time he felt what doomed men must feel, almost as if he were one of those poor desperate animals being led to its death.

Horses pulled coaches, drays, wagons filled with barrels and cases of foodstuffs. Horses hunted, their bodies glistening in the sunlight in the stables at Sandringham or Windsor. Yet those were another breed. These were tired, aged beasts, their mouths smeared with foam, their eyes wild, pulling at the ropes which bound them, startled by the sudden blow of a steel mallet to their skulls, staggering, falling, as the butchers closed in on them, beginning immediately to saw at their flesh, until the walls of the building reeked with death.

Eddy felt each horse's thoughts, the bewilderment, the terror, the suffering agony. He had dreamed of such a place, but had never been inside one.

There were knives everywhere, lying on stools, on the floor. He picked one up. It was a long cutting blade. No one noticed him leave the place, taking the knife with him.

He stood for a long time in front of a cart into which bleeding carcasses were piled. He watched the blood ooze from the fur and the flies gather all over them. At this moment his deaf, unresponsive mother was asleep in St. James's Palace—his father was in the arms of his mistress somewhere on the Continent. His first feelings were rage, then revulsion, then terror that seemed to grab at him, he felt so alone, so sick inside. He touched the edge of the knife, the thick blade in his hand. He smiled as it gave him a sudden sense of power. He gazed up the street at the shadow moving toward him under the streetlight. A long drifting shadow. He waited, holding the knife up under his coat.

Polly Ann Nicholls had finally made it home from the Frying Pan public house in Brick Lane. Staggering a little, her head bent forward, she had reached the lodging house at No. 18 Thrawl

Street, Spitalfields. But the manageress would not let her in. She lacked fourpence for a bed.

"Never mind. I'll soon get my doss money," Polly boasted. "Look what a jolly bonnet I've got now." She pointed to her new straw, trimmed with black velvet.

She headed back into the streets, a pathetic sight in her early forties, a little over five feet tall, her long brown hair almost gray. Poverty and gin had marred any attractiveness she might once have had.

She had been married for several years to William Nicholls, a printer's machinist in Old Kent Road, and had borne him five children. But loneliness had caused her to drink heavily. Her marriage broke up in 1881, Nicholls accusing her of desertion.

In the police courts Polly appealed to Nicholls for child support. Finally, in desperation, she had to move in with her father, a blacksmith in Camberwell. Her drinking continued. At last she abandoned her children and fled to Lambeth Workhouse in Prince's Road, and then to Ingleside, Wandsworth Common, where she managed to get a job as a domestic servant. She was happy for a while, perhaps for the first time in her life, writing to her father of her new domicile, "a grand place with trees and gardens back and front." She added, "My employers are teetotalers and religious, so I ought to get on."

But her craving for drink was too much for her. She stole three pounds from her employers, crossed the Thames, and finally lost herself in the streets of East London.

An hour or so after being refused admittance to the doss house at No. 18 Thrawl Street, Polly encountered Emily Holland, a street whore, on Whitechapel Road. Polly was more drunk than ever and staggered into a brick wall. She admitted to Emily that she had made her doss money three times that day but had spent it on drink. She related in slurring tones that she had been kipping in a doss house in "Flowery Dean Street" where "they slept men as well as women."

Emily tried to persuade her to come home with her, but Polly mumbled that she was going to make another try at raising the price of a bed. As she left Emily, Polly staggered eastward down

Whitechapel Road. Another hundred yards and she could hardly walk at all. She turned up Buck's Row. Passing Barber's Horse Slaughter House, she trembled a little. There was a man in the darkness standing next to one of the carts piled high with bloody carcasses. A tall man with a moustache. Perhaps he would save her from the dark night and send her home to bed.

But as the man drifted toward her, she felt a tug, as if she should move on. She took a step, then stopped beside the curb and beckoned to him. He quickly crossed the short empty street, then smiled. It was the last thing she ever saw—his smile. As the thing in his hand swept forward.

At 3:20 A.M. market porter George Cross turned into Buck's Row on his way to work at Spitalfields Market. He was nearly opposite Barber's Horse Slaughter House when he saw a tarpaulin, at least he thought it was a tarpaulin, lying on the opposite side of the road. He looked closer. What he saw, and had mistaken for a curled-up canvas sheet, was, in fact, Polly Nicholls' body.

He heard footsteps approaching and quickly stepped back into the shadows. He then recognized fellow-porter John Paul coming up the street. "Mate, give us a hand," he called out. "There's a woman lying here but I can't make out whether she's drunk or fainted."

The two men bent over the woman's body. Cross touched her face. It was warm. He lifted her hands. "She's copped it," he murmured, "she's deader'n a haddock."

But John Paul was not convinced. "Come on, mate, let's get her on her feet. She's probably just dead drunk."

Cross drew away. "Not me, I'm not touching her. Come on let's get out of here." With that, the two men took off running down the street.

Moments later, Constable John Neil, on his regular rounds, passed along Buck's Row. Noticing a dark heap on the side of the road, he flashed his lantern in its direction. It was the body of a woman, lying on her back, her eyes wide and staring. Her straw bonnet had been knocked off and lay in the gutter next to her. Bending down, the policeman noticed that she smelled heavily of gin. Supposing she was drunk, he started to raise her. He then discovered that her throat had been slit.

At that moment he heard Constable Haine passing along on his neighboring beat up Brady Street. Police Constable Neil called to him, "Run for Dr. Llewellyn—a woman's been murdered."

The first underground railway in the world opened in 1863, *the year before Eddy was born.* It ran from Paddington to Farringdon Street, a distance of four miles. Its construction was met with extreme opposition. It was prophesied that it would bring St. Paul's Cathedral, Westminster Abbey, and the Houses of Parliament "crashing to the ground." Engineers warned that the tunnels would cave in because of the weight of the traffic in the streets above; houses would be shaken by the vibration of the trains and their inhabitants poisoned by the fumes from the engines.

Punch assailed the notion: "Our modern projectors, having exhausted the old world of railways above ground, have invented a new world of a subterranean kind, in which they propose to construct lines under the present wide leading streets of London . . . The prospectus states that the thing can be accomplished without any serious engineering difficulties. The difficulties, instead of being serious, will, we suppose, be merely laughable."

It was a triumph for Charles Pearson, the City Solicitor, who was responsible for the idea. He had fought to get his plan for an underground railway accepted, and then fought to find the money for it. Unfortunately, Pearson died in 1862, a year before his dream was fulfilled.

The Circle Line was completed in October 1884. It never was a separate line in the sense that it had its own tracks. The northern part, Gloucester Road to Aldgate via Baker Street, was built in sections by the Metropolitan Railway, and the southern portion was constructed by the District Railway. These two separate companies, although cooperating in this instance, were extremely antagonistic to each other. One of their main objectives was a race to build a circular underground railway—which would be known as the Inner Circle.

Since 1886 the eastern terminus of the District Railway had been Whitechapel Station, located two blocks from Buck's Row.

At first, trains did not arrive or depart from Whitechapel at regular intervals, but, with the trains to and from New Cross, they provided an approximate ten- to fifteen-minute service west of Aldgate East.

Gradually, there were four trains an hour departing from Whitechapel on Monday to Friday, with an approximate half-hourly service in the early morning, late evening, and on Sunday. From there, it was a ten-to-fifteen-minute ride to Mansion House. The line was not actually underground but was "cut and cover" in construction. The road having been closed to traffic, a trench was dug and lined with brickwork, and then brickwork arches were built and the road was relaid. Trains were hauled by steam locomotives using coke, made from the finest Durham coal, which was burned in ovens for several hours in order to deprive it of every trace of sulfur and other objectionable exhalation.

Still, journeys were often a nightmare, the carriages were dirty and dark, being lighted only by small gas jets. Everywhere, suffocating fumes took the place of fresh air. Occasionally, if someone wanted to read, they found it advisable to bring a candle and stick it on the side of the car.

Eddy boarded the first train departing from Whitechapel Station at 5:36 A.M. It was virtually empty but he sat in as dark a corner of the coach as he could find. He still clutched the knife under his coat. He would be home in a few minutes.

Chapter 2

THE RITUAL

Friedrich Wilhelm, Crown Prince of Prussia, had long been beloved by the British public and was especially admired by his brother-in-law, the Prince of Wales. In fact, their friendship ran so deeply that Friedrich's son Prince Wilhelm, feeling left out, resented it. He complained that when he was with the two men, the Prince of Wales overlooked him completely. Prince Wilhelm's animosity toward his British uncle continued into his reign as Kaiser of the German Empire, which began that August of 1888.

During the funeral of his father, whose reign as Friedrich III had been for about three months, the twenty-nine-year-old Wilhelm treated the Prince of Wales with contempt. Referring to him as "the Old Peacock" (the Prince of Wales was in fact forty-six), the young Kaiser-to-be snubbed and ignored him.

Germany was ruled by Prince Otto von Bismarck, who was Chancellor but the young Kaiser was already moving to dismiss him and govern the Empire himself. He was surrounded by a coterie of ambitious young men, and he now planned politically to involve himself in the Balkans, Asiatic Turkey, and Africa.

The Prince of Wales was disturbed by his nephew's expansionist ambitions and mockingly referred to him as "Wilhelm the Great." But there was no way that he could counter the young Kaiser's insults and abuses, which even extended to Queen Victoria, whom Wilhelm openly referred to as "the old hag."

The strife between the English and German Royal Houses was further precipitated by the Prince of Wales's defense of the Duke of Cumberland, son and heir to the last King of Hanover, who fought on the losing side during the Austro-Prussian War of 1866 and consequently had lost his kingdom and fortune to Prussia. While attending the funeral of Friedrich III, the Prince of Wales had asked Prince Otto von Bismarck's son Herbert an embarrassing question: If Kaiser Friedrich had lived, would Germany have made concessions on the questions of Alsace-Lorraine, North Schleswig, and the Duke of Cumberland's estates? The question was repeated to Kaiser Wilhelm, who angrily replied in a speech describing the Prince of Wales's inquiry as an intolerable insult, and affirming that his father would never have yielded what the Prussian sword had won.

This bitter feud between the Prince and the Kaiser stirred the leaders of Europe to both sides, and the Prince of Wales was attacked by the newspapers of Germany. In the weeks following Friedrich's funeral, he stayed away from London, continuing his tour of the Continent in the company of his favorite mistress, Lady Brooke. Meanwhile, his wife, Alexandra, who had refused to go to Germany because of her dislike of the Prussians, remained at Marlborough House.

Politically, England was facing a violent upheaval from within. Queen Victoria had made a disastrous choice in appointing a former Major General of the Royal Engineers, Charles Warren, as Metropolitan Police Commissioner. Warren, who wore a thick, heavy moustache and a monocle screwed into his right eye, was often pictured regaled in full dress uniform, sitting on a horse, wearing an old-fashioned policeman's chimney-pot hat. He was a military man who had little sensitivity for handling domestic problems. He reorganized Scotland Yard like a military barracks, staffing it with army officers in executive posts. He surrounded himself with "brass" but had few police officers on the streets. At one point, he had 168 inspectors, 196 sergeants, but only 89 constables on duty. His ineptitude had reached its culmination during the bloody riot which occurred on Sunday, November 13, 1887.

When a crowd of unemployed Londoners, numbering twenty thousand, carrying banners inscribed with Scriptural texts, converged on Trafalgar Square to demonstrate, Warren met them with a force of four thousand soldiers armed with fixed bayonets. The confrontation was a pitched battle of clubbing and gunfire. Within a few minutes, two hundred demonstrators were carried off to nearby hospitals and there were at least two known deaths. *The Times* the following morning devoted eight and a half columns to reporting the incident.

"Bloody Sunday" earned Charles Warren the bitter hatred of London's working class population, but he was feted by the aristocracy for his firm handling of the situation. Shortly thereafter he was knighted.

For the London policemen, however, the event had tragic consequences. Citizens who had respected the city's constables now regarded them with suspicion and contempt.

Police Surgeon, Dr. Rees Ralph Llewellyn, was thoroughly annoyed at having been awakened from sleep. When he arrived in Buck's Row at 4 A.M. on the morning of August 31, 1888, he viewed with distaste the curiosity seekers who had begun to mill around Polly Nicholls' body. The murdered woman was lying on her back with her legs stiff as if the killer had arranged her in a formal pose. Her throat had been cut from ear to ear, severing the carotid arteries, but there was little blood, "not more than would fill two wineglasses, or half a pint at the outside," Dr. Llewellyn noted. She was clad in a rusty brown ulster with seven large brass buttons, a dark linsey dress, two flannel petticoats, each stenciled with the words "Lambeth Workhouse," and a pair of close-ribbed brown stays. On her feet she wore black woolen stockings and elas-

tic-sided ankle-length boots. The police had found only two possessions on her body: a black comb and a broken piece of looking
glass.

As there were no mortuaries close by, Dr. Llewellyn ordered the
body be taken to a workhouse in Old Montague Street. There,
when her tightly laced stays were cut apart, he discovered that
Polly Nicholls had been disemboweled. He later commented to
the press: "I have seen many terrible cases, but none so brutal as
this."

The killer's knife had been driven into the lower left part of her
abdomen and then propelled in a frenzied-like fashion all the way
up as far as the diaphragm. Dr. Llewellyn remarked that it was a
deep gash, completely cutting through the tissue. There were several incisions spearing across the abdomen, as well as three or four
jabs running downward on the right side. All had been performed
with a long-bladed knife, fairly sharp, used with intense, violent
strokes.

An inquest was scheduled for Saturday morning, September 1,
at the Working Lads' Institute in Whitechapel Road. When the
doors opened, there was a rush for seats by the curious public who
thronged the street outside. The proceedings were presided over
by Wynn E. Baxter, coroner for the northeastern division of
Middlesex County. He was a legal expert and a dandy, who wore
to the hearing "white and checked trousers, a dazzling white waist-
coat, a crimson scarf and a dark coat," according to the *East London Observer*, attributing the reason for his gaudy attire to his
having just returned from a tour of Scandinavia. The witnesses at
the inquest included George Cross, the market porter who had
first discovered the body, Police Constable Neil, who was the
officer on the scene, and three butchers, employed at Barber's
Slaughter House, who testified they had heard no cries or sounds
of a scuffle. Finally, William Nicholls, printer's machinist and the
deceased's estranged husband, appeared. He was a small, pale man
with a full brown beard. He had rented mourning clothes—a tall
silk hat, black frock coat, black tie, and dark flannel trousers—for
the occasion. He explained that his former wife had been an alco-
holic. "She deserted me four or five times, if not six," he insisted,

"and the last time she left me with five children, the youngest of whom was only sixteen months old."

Dr. Rees Ralph Llewellyn was then called upon to give his view of how the murder had been performed. He began by saying that he felt the murderer had held his hand pressed against the victim's mouth and the knife was then used, possibly by a left-handed person. The weapon itself had been a pointed weapon with a stout back, such as a cork cutter's or a shoemaker's knife. He carefully avoided alluding to the more obvious butcher's knife which would have cast immediate suspicion onto the workers employed by Barber's Horse Slaughter House.

Coroner Wynn E. Baxter then rose and thanked the committee of the Working Lads' Institute for the use of their room. "Otherwise," he went on, "we would have been forced to hold this inquest in the parlor of a public house." His closing remarks suddenly erupted into a diatribe citing the lack of mortuary facilities in East London. As if entirely forgetting the deceased Polly Nicholls, he vehemently attacked the sanitary authorities for their lack of interest in the situation. "Surely if mortuaries are found necessary in the West End, there must be stronger reasons for them here in the midst of so much squalid crowding!"

Coroner Baxter's remarks were like a signal. The jury foreman leaped up and condemned the Home Secretary, Henry Matthews, for not instantly offering a reward for the killer. "You can bet that a substantial reward would have been offered if it had been a rich person murdered." The inflamed juror then jerked twenty-five pounds from his pocket and announced that he would offer it himself for the murderer's capture. "After all," he exclaimed, "poor people have souls like anybody else!"

The London press had already highlighted the murder in Buck's Row, and by Sunday morning it was being discussed everywhere. There had been a similar trail of unsolved murders since Police Commissioner Charles Warren's appointment, but none so savage or unexplainable as Polly Nicholls'. Coroner Baxter's remarks were a further indication that the authorities, because of ineptitude or lack of caring, were incapable of dealing with the situation. The clamor of rebellion was slowly stirring as all eyes became fixed on the funeral of Polly Nicholls. A polished elm coffin containing her remains was carted to Ilford Cemetery in the presence of her father and three of her children. Her husband, William Nicholls, once again in hired mourning clothes, rode in a separate coach. Finally, a week later, because of the influx of ghoulish sightseers at the murder scene, the residents of Buck's Row successfully petitioned to have the street's name changed to Durward Street. It was a temporary escape from the bloody circumstance which now had all of London restless for the killer's capture.

James Monro, the Assistant Police Commissioner and head of C.I.D., had resigned on August 31, 1888, after a serious quarrel with Sir Charles Warren. Monro, a brilliant officer, had long objected to Warren's attempts to enforce a military regime at Scotland Yard. His resignation left a serious gap in the policing of East London and it left the detective branch without an effective head.

His successor, Robert Anderson, was a socialite barrister who had no experience in police work. On September 8, his first day on the job, Anderson left the city even less protected as he embarked by train for a month's holiday in Switzerland.

Early the same morning, Prince Eddy had stolen a leather butcher's apron from a Jewish abattoir in Aldgate High Street. He had watched with fascination how the animals were prepared for slaughter: their legs tied with ropes, as a quick forward and backward stroke with a knife cut their throats to the bone. Next, an incision was made in the chest exposing the heart and lungs, and finally the stomachs were cut open to release the intestines and kidneys. With intense interest he watched the Jewish ritual slaughtermen for several hours before heading into the streets of Spitalfields.

Remembering how the butchers in the Horse Slaughter House in Buck's Row had all worn white neckerchiefs stained with blood about their necks, Eddy, before leaving home, had tied a bright red bandanna around his throat. He wore the same dark overcoat that he had worn the evening of August 31. Under his arm, tightly wrapped in a copy of the *Daily Telegraph,* he carried the knife.

He turned up Commercial Road and wandered along it past a row of dingy saloons and pubs. Several women beckoned to him but the neighborhood was still too noisy and crowded. It was a warm dark morning with a slight fog in the air. He had read with delight the accounts of the first murder opposite Barber's Horse Slaughter House. But tonight he would outdo that performance. He needed a willing victim and a more private place to work. He would not choose the street this time, perhaps an alley or a court-yard.

He bypassed the flood of teeming lodging houses along Thrawl Street, Flower-and-Dean, and Fashion Street. Crossing Dorset Street, he stopped opposite the corner of Hanbury.

The woman standing beside a brown brick building was his mother's height, no more than five feet tall. She had brown wavy hair and pale white skin. She beckoned to him with a willing smile that meant she would go anywhere, do anything he desired. As he drew closer, he noticed that her breath reeked of stale gin.

He removed his red bandanna and tied it around her neck. Then he took some coins from his pocket and slid them into her hand.

"Will you?" he asked.

"Yes," she quietly replied.

She seemed robust and well proportioned, perhaps forty or so, fairly attractive, and as she opened her mouth, Eddy noticed that she was missing two front teeth.

As she reached up to touch his face, Eddy quickly added, "Somewhere private."

She nodded, then smiled, as she gestured for him to follow.

She led him a short way down Hanbury Street into a building passageway. At the end of the passageway down a few steps was a yard. As she led Eddy into the deserted yard, he closed the wooden passageway door behind him.

Through the darkness he watched her lean against the wooden fence and begin to pull up her skirts. Eddy removed his coat, revealing the leather butcher's apron tied around his waist. She stared at him a second, obviously trying to make out what he was up to. Playfully at first, he reached to her throat, grabbing the red bandanna. Then he let the knife slide out of the newspaper.

The woman gave a sudden grunt, and in terror began to push at him. As she tried to shove him away, with one hand clutching the bandanna, Eddy dropped the knife and hit her in the face with all his might.

She reeled back against the fence. He hit her a second time. Twisting the bandanna knot tighter, it seemed to take several minutes before her choking stopped. Then she suddenly sank backward.

Picking up the knife and leveling it at her throat, he hacked back and forth twice until the blade touched bone.

He could feel her wet blood all over his hands as he lay her down near the steps where there was more light. Tearing open the collar of her dress, he drove the knife into her chest, revealing her heart and lungs, and then with another thrust he ripped open her stomach.

John Davis, an elderly lodger who lived at 29 Hanbury Street, rose from his bed at about five forty-five and, still dressing himself, came downstairs as the Christ Church clock began to strike 6 A.M. The door to the yard was shut. He pushed it open, and there in the early dawn light he saw the body of Annie Chapman.

Overcome with revulsion, his trouser belt still in his hands, Davis stumbled down the passageway into the street. He cried out to some workmen nearby, but his face was so stricken that none of them dared enter the passageway.

Inspector Joseph Chandler was on duty when he saw the workmen running up Hanbury Street toward him. He hurried to the passageway and pushed back the wooden door.

The woman was lying on her back near the fence. Her hands were raised with the palms upward. Her coat and skirt were pushed up over her bloodstained stockings. She had been disemboweled.

From the windows overlooking the yard, dozens of spectators watched as Inspector Chandler searched the yard. It was an area about ten by fourteen feet, half-paved with broken flagstones and torn pieces of wood. Chandler discovered bloodstains on the fence about fourteen inches above the ground. The only other bloodstains were on the back wall of the house near the head of the body.

Divisional surgeon Dr. George Bagster Phillips arrived a few minutes later. Twenty years' practical experience had qualified him as one of the most able scientists on the Metropolitan Police Force. Phillips carefully examined the woman's body and jotted his findings in a notebook:

> Lying on her back, dead, left arm resting on left breast, legs drawn up, abducted, small intestines and flap of the abdomen lying on right side above right shoulder attached by a cord with the rest of the intestines inside the body; two flaps of skin from the lower part of the abdomen lying in a large quantity of blood above the left shoulder; throat cut deeply from left and back in a jagged manner right around the throat.

He also noted that there was a handkerchief knotted around the neck and that the victim's throat had been severed so savagely that her head had almost been lopped from the body.

But it was his search of the yard and the area near the body that turned up certain unusual clues. Several items had been deliberately placed near the victim: her only possessions, a piece of muslin, a comb and a paper case, had been cut from one of the pockets of her dress. In addition, two rings had been torn from her fingers and had been positioned with some pennies and two new farthings at the woman's feet. It was as if the killer had engaged in some private ritual, or perhaps had made it look that way in order to tantalize the police.

Finally, at one end of the yard, a few inches from a water tap, Dr. Phillips discovered a leather butcher's apron saturated with water.

Chapter 3

THE DEMON IN THE SHADOWS

John Pizer was thirty-three, a Polish Jew employed in White-chapel as a shoemaker. When Detective Sergeant William Thicke, of H Division, arrived at his house in Whitechapel in the company of three officers, Pizer opened the door to them. Thicke immediately grabbed Pizer by the collar, announcing, "You're just the man I want." He then charged the shoemaker with the murder of Annie Chapman. Searching his rooms, he found five sharp, long-handled knives.

Pizer's arrest had threatening consequences for the Jewish population of Whitechapel. Within hours, scores of unfortunate Jews were harassed and beaten in the streets. In describing the sudden surge of anti-Semitism, the *Daily News* warned: "There may soon be murders from panic to add to murders from lust for blood . . . a touch will fire the whole district in the mood in which it is now." The paper went on to report that Dr. George Bagster Phillips, the divisional police surgeon, and his assistant "were out of their beds nearly all Saturday night in attendance on cases of assault, some of them of the most serious character, arising

directly or indirectly out of the intense excitement occasioned by
the discussion of the murder." No Jew was safe. Pizer was pictured by the press as having "piercing eyes" and when he walked
it was "noiselessly like a cat." In his trade as shoemaker, he often
wore a leather apron and he did, by necessity, handle sharp-
pointed knives.

But Pizer, who resided with his elderly stepmother and his
brother, Gabriel, was of a delicate nature. In truth, he could not
be classified as a run-of-the-mill shoemaker. He designed and
fashioned ballet slippers.

One might assume that he would have chosen to slay ballerinas,
rather than prostitutes, but such subtleties were easily lost on the
mobs in Whitechapel joyously celebrating his capture. A broad-
sheet was hawked in the streets announcing

> *They've captured Leather Apron now,*
> *if guilty you'll agree;*
> *He'll have to meet a murderer's doom,*
> *and hang upon a tree.*

At the bottom, it blatantly described the details of his capture:

> At nine o'clock this morning Detective Sergeant William Thicke,
> H Division, who has had charge of this case, succeeded in captur-
> ing the man known as Leather Apron. There is no doubt that he
> is the murderer, for a large number of long-bladed knives were
> found in his possession.

The *East London Observer* added to the Victorian taste for
melodrama by describing the Jew as:

> 5 ft. 4 ins. tall with a dark-hued face, which was not altogether
> pleasant to look upon by reason of grizzly black strips of hair,
> nearly an inch in length, which almost covered the face. The thin
> lips, too, had a cruel, sardonic look . . .

But as the facts emerged, it was discovered that Pizer had an
unshakable alibi. He had been home in his rooms at the time of
Annie Chapman's murder on the morning of September 8.

The mob at once turned its attention to another Jew named
Jacobs, who worked in the slaughterhouse in Aldgate High Street.

After being questioned by the police, he was pointed out as the Whitechapel killer. He was stoned in the streets and had to flee to the nearest police station in order to save his life. After several such incidents, he lost his reason and had to be committed to an asylum.

Police were soon arresting suspects in droves. Fourteen were held at the Commercial Street station alone, while others were dragged into the Leman Street and Upper Thames Street stations for interrogation.

On Monday, September 10, in order to protect themselves, sixteen Jewish tradesmen met at the Crown Club on Mile End Road to form the Whitechapel Vigilance Committee. The vigilantes included a cigar manufacturer, a tailor, a picture-frame maker, and a butcher. A local merchant, George Lusk, was chosen as their chairman. Admittedly, they had no idea how to apprehend the murderer that the press now referred to as "Leather Apron," but they adopted a resolution born of tremendous desperation:

> Finding that in spite of the murders being committed in our midst the police force is inadequate to discover the author or authors of the late atrocities, we, the undersigned, have formed ourselves into a committee and intend offering a substantial reward to anyone, citizen or otherwise, who shall give such information as will be the means of bringing the murderer or murderers to justice.

Although they emphasized a "substantial" reward, they were, in fact, unable to collect more than £200 for their purpose. Finally, they were forced to use the money to hire two private detectives, in addition to paying a dozen unemployed men to patrol the streets of Whitechapel from midnight until 5 A.M.

Public reaction to the killings was soon aimed at American actor Richard Mansfield, who quickly decided to withdraw his successful version of *Dr. Jekyll and Mr. Hyde* from the boards of the Lyceum after only a ten-week run. His action was commended by the *Daily Telegraph*: "Experience has taught this clever young actor that there is no taste in London just now for horrors on the stage. There is quite sufficient to make us shudder out of doors."

45

Hysteria was rampant. And it soon reached its crescendo with the arrest of another suspect believed to be the killer.

In Gravesend, William Henry Piggott was found wandering in a dazed state with bloodstains on his clothing and his hands badly mutilated. Piggott told the police that while walking along Brick Lane on the morning of the murder, he saw a woman convulsed in a fit. When he attempted to help her up, she bit his hand. Recoiling in anger, he struck the woman, who began to scream. He fled from the scene as two policeman started after him.

Chief Inspector Frederick Abberline took Piggott into custody and when they arrived at London Bridge Station he forced Piggott to crouch on the floor of the cab in order to save him from a mob who had gathered in the streets outside. Abberline's precautions were in vain. The news had already spread that Piggott was the Whitechapel killer. The mob began to shout threats as Abberline approached the station with his prisoner.

Once inside the station, Piggott became incoherent, and the divisional police surgeon was called in. Although Piggott was cleared of the murders, he was certified as insane and committed to an asylum at Bow.

Dozens of men, both intoxicated and sober, walked into police stations and confessed to the murders. The disembowelment of Annie Chapman had touched a manic chord of guilt and exhibitionism within the citizenry that left the police exhausted and stupefied. To add to the confusion, the police themselves manufactured a description of the killer in order to try to convince the panic-stricken populace that they were doing their job:

> Description of a man who entered a passage of the house at which murder was committed of a prostitute at 2 a.m. on 8th— Age 37; height, 5 ft. 7 ins.; rather dark beard and moustache. Dress—shirt, dark jacket, dark vest and trousers, black scarf, and black felt hat. Spoke with a foreign accent.

The fact that no witnesses had seen the murderer, nor heard him speak, made their attempt laughable. However, the "foreign accent" element pandered to the prejudices latent in the Victorian sensibility that no Englishman could possibly have committed such a crime.

Again, Coroner Wynne E. Baxter opened the inquest proceedings at the Working Lads' Institute by severely criticizing the authorities in charge. They had not furnished him with a diagram of the murder scene, nor even a plan of the house located at 29 Hanbury Street. "If country police can do this for a coroner, surely the Metropolitan Police can do the same," he reflected.

The first witness to testify was the victim's friend Amelia Farmer. On the Monday prior to her murder, Annie had complained of not feeling well. She had been involved in a street brawl with another prostitute, Liza Cooper, and as a result had suffered a blackened eye and a badly bruised chest.

Their fight had been over a piece of soap which Annie had borrowed from Liza, and then refused to return. When Liza insulted her, Annie had slapped Liza's face, and threatened: "Think yourself lucky I did not do more."

With that, Liza beat her to the ground and when Amelia Farmer met Annie the following day, she was hobbling in pain. She had had nothing to eat or drink that day, except a cup of tea, so Amelia gave her twopence and warned her not to have any drink.

Three days later, when Amelia again met her, Annie was still recovering from her injuries. She told Amelia, "It's no use my giving way. I must pull myself together and go out and get some money or I shall have no lodgings." It was the last time Amelia saw Annie Chapman alive.

Witness Timothy Donovan recalled how on the night of the murder Annie had begged him for a bed in his lodging house at 35 Dorset Street, although she admitted that she had no money. He replied by reminding her that she knew the rules and that she could not stay without paying. When she left at 2 A.M. on the morning of September 8, she asked him not to let her bed, which was still unoccupied, as she would soon be back.

At 5:15 A.M. on the morning of the murder, Albert Cadoche, a carpenter who lived next door to the house at 29 Hanbury Street, testified that he paid a visit to the outhouse in the backyard of his premises. As he passed the five-foot-six-inch wooden fence which separated the two yards, he heard a woman's voice cry out, "No, no." On returning from the outhouse, he had overheard a struggle and then a hard thud, as if someone had fallen against the fence. Not wishing to interfere, Mr. Cadoche stated that he returned to his room without investigating the incident.

Dr. George Baxter Phillips took the stand and described the murder weapon as "a very sharp knife, with a thin, narrow blade . . . at least six inches or eight inches in length, probably longer." He refused, however, to give a description of the mutilations, explaining that it "could only be painful to the feelings of the jury and the public."

Coroner Baxter would not accept Dr. Phillips' reticence. He demanded that the police surgeon describe the wounds in full.

> DR. PHILLIPS: I still think it is a great pity that I should have to give this evidence.
>
> BAXTER: We are here to decide the cause of death and therefore have a right to hear all particulars. Whether this evidence is made public or not rests with the press. I might add that I have never before heard of any evidence being kept back from a coroner.
>
> DR. PHILLIPS: I am in the hands of the court. But what I was going to detail took place *after death*.
>
> BAXTER: That is a matter of opinion.

Dr. Phillips then requested that the room be cleared of all women and boys as he began to describe the results of his examination which *The Times*, the following morning, regarded as "totally unfit for publication."

Coroner Baxter concluded the inquest proceedings by describing the murder as being performed "with cool impudence and reckless daring." Picturing the "Judas-like" manner with which the victim was approached, he commented: "Nothing is more noticeable than the emptying of her pockets and the arrangement of their contents with businesslike precision near her feet."

But there was one chilling bit of information that even Dr.

Baxter had been reluctant to mention. Finally he brought it forth like an exploding bombshell over his listeners. In examining the victim's mutilated body, something was found missing. Annie Chapman's uterus.

Vacationing in Switzerland, Robert Anderson, the newly appointed head of the C.I.D, came up with a suggestion to end the murders. Every prostitute found loitering in Whitechapel after midnight should be arrested. He argued that it was the only course "merciful to the very small class of women affected."

His superior, Commissioner Charles Warren, already under attack from both press and citizenry, quickly rejected the idea. A rumor had been circulating that Warren was about to be assigned to a post in Africa in order to reduce the government's embarrassment, and this was picked up as a source of satire by the *Pall Mall Gazette* who suggested that he be made Warden of the Marshes of Upper Zambesi in order to fend off Arab slave-traders. In a more serious tone, the *Daily Telegraph* charged that Scotland Yard was "in an utterly hopeless and worthless condition," citing "the scandalous exhibition of stupidity and ineptitude revealed at the East-end inquests."

The Times, meanwhile, had a theory as to the murderer's identity:

> He is a man lodging in a comparatively decent house in the district, to which he would be able to retire quickly, and in which, once it was reached, he would be able at his leisure to remove from his person all traces of his hideous crime. It is at any rate almost certain that the murderer would not have ventured to return to a common lodging-house smeared with blood as he must have been.

Moralists and reformers such as the Reverend Samuel Barnett, Vicar of St. Jude's, Whitechapel, believed that more murders were "bound to come," that they were the result of a "generation in lawless intercourse." And the *East London Advertiser* reflected that as the result of such "revolting acts of blood . . . the mind turns as it were instinctively to some theory of occult force, and the myths of the Dark Ages arise before the imagination. Ghouls, vampires, blood-suckers . . ."

"The real criminal," cried out the socialist journal *Justice*, "is the vicious bourgeois system which, based upon class injustice, condemns thousands to poverty, vice, and crime."

Meanwhile, dwellers who were able to look out over the back of 29 Hanbury Street from their windows, did a brisk business charging sightseers for a view of the yard where "the Chapman 'orror" had been committed.

Chapter 4

THE LETTERS

James Stephen hated women. In the book of poems he was preparing for publication, like his idol Swinburne he made no attempt to conceal this obsession.

> *If all the harm that women have done*
> *Were put in a bundle and rolled into one,*
> *Earth would not hold it,*
> *The sky could not enfold it,*
> *It could not be lighted nor warmed by the sun;*
> *Such masses of evil*
> *Would puzzle the devil*
> *And keep him in fuel while Time's wheels run.*

The poem was titled "A Thought," and James Stephen obviously had many such thoughts.

It was an irrational hatred, not born of rejection. James was one of London's handsomest young bachelors. But he had an immature sense that women were responsible for the downfall of men.

Such feelings were common in Victorian England. The whorish

element was exploited in its literature and indeed became a source of unending anxiety. T. H. Lecky, the nineteenth-century reformer, resolved that prostitutes were "the eternal priestesses of humanity" within whom were "concentrated the passions that have filled the world with shame." And D'Annunzio, in his novel *L'Invincible,* explored the image through an inner dialogue:

> "Cruelty lurks hidden in her love," he thought. "There is something destructive in her, which becomes the more evident the more violent her orgasm."

"Cruelty," "destructive"—these were terms with which the rational Victorian could hardly deal. Acts of passion were kept camouflaged beneath exquisite gestures, manners, sentiments. Sex, in itself, was harmful and offensive.

It was not that the Victorians did not indulge in sex, the Bishop of Exeter estimated that there were eighty thousand prostitutes in London, while Henry Mayhew retorted that the Bishop's estimate was "below the reality rather than above it." But there was a perversity in Victorian thinking that equated the sexual act with the flowering of evil. Since rules and restrictions did not allow one to love freely, the purely physical act became synonymous with defilement.

Finally, it was Swinburne's uncontrolled romanticism which released in the Victorian mind the full violence of this passion:

> *Stretch your throat out that I may kiss all round*
> *Where mine shall be cut through: suppose my mouth*
> *The axe-edge to bite so sweet a throat in twain*
> *With bitter iron, should not it turn soft*
> *As lip is soft to lip?*

Even the artist Aubrey Beardsley, inspired by the Whitechapel murders, was moved to express in poetry what he could not convey on canvas:

> *He snatched a bottle of Cologne,*
> *And broke the neck between his hands.*
> *The Princess gave a little scream,*
> *Carrousel's cut was sharp and deep;*

He left her softly as a dream
That leaves a sleeper to his sleep;
He left the room on pointed feet,
Smiling that things had gone so well.
They hanged him in Meridian Street.
You pray in vain for Carrousel.

As the Victorians prided themselves on being God-fearing, their suppressed fascination took on religious overtones. Wilde's *Salome* conjured up elements of uncontrollable desire, coupled once again with the destructive element inherent in all women, that cruelty which "lurks hidden in her love" inevitably eventuating in violence. To which James Stephen added his own brooding interpretation:

In days of old there lived a maid;
She was the mistress of her trade;
A prostitute of high repute—
The Harlot of Jerusalem.

James then pictured a student who calls on this woman:

One night returning from a spree,
With customary whore-lust he
Made up his mind to call and see
The Harlot of Jerusalem.

The student's advances toward her were prefaced by a verse which in any age would be considered obscene:

It was for her no fortune good,
That he should need to root his pud,
And choose her out of the brood
Of Harlots of Jerusalem.

Describing the student as a "syphilitic spawn of hell," James pictured the woman's fetishistic rape at the student's hands:

He leaned the whore against the slum,
And tied her at the knee and bum.

53

By the end of the poem, the whore has contracted syphilis from the student, and an Onanite passing by adds to the destructive pattern:

> *So when he saw the grunting pair,*
> *With roars of rage he rent the air,*
> *And vowed that he would soon take care*
> *Of the Harlot of Jerusalem.*

How different was James Stephen from his cousin Leslie, who had written:

> Respectability has spread its leaden mantle over the whole country, and the man wins the race who can worship that great goddess with the most undivided attention.

On the surface, James *appeared* extremely respectable, being the grandson of Sir James Stephen, Professor of Modern History at Cambridge. His father, James Fitzjames Stephen, was a prominent judge, and it seemed inevitable that James would have an illustrious career in whatever field he chose to pursue.

When Eddy entered Cambridge in 1883, James was chosen to replace Reverend Dalton as the young heir's tutor. But in a short time, James introduced Eddy to other pursuits as well.

He surrounded him with a circle of homosexual companions, including Harry Wilson, Oscar Browning, and Edmund Gosse, but continued to guide Eddy's progress himself, while writing of the young man's faults to Reverend Dalton: "I do not think he can probably derive much benefit from lectures at Cambridge—he hardly knows the meaning of the words *to read.*"

It was control that James was after, for as tutor to the future King, he took his place as an immediate celebrity.

Eddy resided in two sets of rooms on the top floor of the last staircase opposite the library of Nevile's Court. A fellow classmate described the setting:

> Nevile's Court, in spite of the tasteless reparations of Essex, has a look of old-world dignity about it, with the great façade of Wren's noble library at one end and the College Hall, from which two flights of shallow steps with balustrades descend to the

level of the glass ploy, at the other. It is the chosen abode of dons and scholars . . .

A Blüthner concert grand piano was installed in Eddy's living quarters, and James invited Cambridge's most skillful musicians to perform for the Prince.

Instead of joining the University's most select clubs, the Pitt and the Athenaeum, Eddy became a member of the Amateur Dramatic Society, to which James belonged. He soon became totally dependent on James and embraced his opinions and judgment. James, in return, selected all of Eddy's friends and jealously guarded him.

Eddy's one interest was playing cards and with James's guidance he became excellent at whist. James also hosted quiet parties at which Eddy was the guest of honor. These were intimate "greek" (the academic sobriquet for "queer") affairs, and as fellow homosexual Harry Wilson described:

> It was delightful to witness the unaffected courtesy and deference which the Prince displayed to older men, and especially to the distinguished scholar who was entertaining him.

But it was in personal matters that Eddy turned to James more than anyone else. For the first time, he had found someone who loved him.

James Stephen was even successful in duping the Prince of Wales into turning against Eddy's former tutor. Lady Geraldine Somerset recorded that the Prince of Wales now talked "of how right alas! our judgement of stupid Dalton was, who taught Prince Eddy *absolutely nothing!*" Unfortunately, the Prince of Wales and his friends were oblivious to James Stephen's corruptive influence over Eddy, but were more impressed by the opinion of one of Eddy's teachers who found himself "astonished how much he has got on with him and thinks, under the circumstances, his papers are infinitely better than he dared to expect." Eddy's progress was attributed to James Stephen's guidance. There seemed little doubt that Eddy was developing a whole new side to his personality.

He accompanied his parents on a state visit to Ireland in April 1885. There they were met by the loyalists with great respect and enthusiasm, and Princess Alexandra visited Trinity College, where she received an honorary Doctor of Music degree. She wrote to Prince George of the ceremony: "I don't think any Irishmen here would do us any harm; they are all nice and friendly." However, when they arrived at Cork, they were descended upon by a mob of Irish nationalists waving black flags and shouting obscenities. Rotten vegetables were thrown at the royal carriage, which moved through the streets under a shower of bricks and garbage. Arthur Ellis, who accompanied the Royal Family, described the experience as "like a bad dream. No one who went through this day will ever forget it . . . streets filled with sullen faces, hideous, cruel countenances, hissing and grimacing . . ." But it was the vilely insulting women that made such a strong impression on Eddy that he described them in a letter to James. He was already forming an intense hatred for such women, and, in time, they would cease to appear to him as women at all, but as fearful forces to be dealt with mercilessly and with the utmost savagery. His father, the Prince of Wales, was described by Ellis as showing "the greatest calmness and courage." And, outwardly, Eddy made no display of the emotions he would one day release.

Upon leaving Cambridge later that year, Eddy was sent by his father to join the 10th Hussars. There he was miserable under the grueling discipline and constantly turned to James for comfort and reassurance. He was now forced to behave like a prince, attending state functions, dinners, and even distributing athletic prizes.

Two years later, he was finally freed from the army and reunited with James at Cambridge, where Eddy received an honorary Doctor of Laws degree. Harry Wilson wrote him a poem, prophesying the glory of Eddy's future:

> *For you, the Prince of this dear Isle,*
> *The loftiest destiny awaits,*
> *To see yon realm's unnumbered states*
> *Conjoined in one. May Heaven smile*

Upon that great, that glorious aim!
And like her Edwards Third and First,
May you, for England's weal athirst,
Add lustre to a royal name.

But Eddy's destiny lay elsewhere. He was to be chillingly remembered by those few who were to learn of his fanatical pursuits and were ultimately forced to keep his secret to themselves. To them it would become more a curse than an allegiance, as they became responsible for shielding the most horrible murderer in England's history. But was Eddy, in fact, much different from Richard III, who allegedly annihilated the innocent offspring of his eldest brother, or Queen Mary, who imprisoned her sister Elizabeth in the Tower of London? The times were different and the motives were no longer political. But this young man, in another time, might have transferred his savage impulses to members of his own family had his ambitions to become King been frustrated. Instead, a dark madness led him into the streets of Whitechapel to annihilate women he did not know. Except to him, they represented all women, as his desire for satisfaction was convoluted into an intense passion to dissect them.

On the morning of September 9, 1888, Eddy arrived at James Stephen's house at 32 De Vere Gardens, Kensington. James had been reading with fascination the details of Annie Chapman's murder when Eddy entered his chambers carrying a package. As if like a child going to his father for approval, Eddy opened the package and laid the contents before his closest, most intimate friend. James Stephen immediately recognized the bloody portion of a human body.

It made him laugh at first, like at some practical joke, and yet he had never known Eddy's humor to descend to the prankster stage.

Eddy did not laugh. His brooding eyes and thin face stared back at James uneasily, yet with extreme seriousness. He wanted James to know what he had done. No one else knew. There was no one he could tell.

He had murdered two women, two common women who had approached him in the stews of Spitalfields.

The first woman had been staggering up the street near a horse slaughterhouse off Whitechapel Road. He had killed her in a sudden moment of agony within himself, that released itself so suddenly—and he knew that no one would find out—

But the second woman was the one he had intended to kill because he wanted suddenly to let everyone know the agony and pain he felt inside. There was something he had found with that woman, better than making love to anyone, a violent act of destruction that had no meaning other than that he felt afterward tremblingly afraid, yet wonderfully free, as if that person were part of himself, some awful burning part that he could cut out and leave there.

But the world would not understand. How could anyone understand the emotions of agony, then release, unless they had known them firsthand as he had.

James had poured them into his poems—the frustration, the heartsick fear, the helplessness. And Eddy had merely expressed these feelings so completely and so utterly for the first time, but there was no going back. James, at first, did not believe the story. Eddy had been reading the newspapers and had imagined it. Perhaps it was hallucination or momentary fantasy. There were people all over London confessing to the murders. Something perhaps had snapped inside Eddy. Yet as he stared at the fragment of humanity in the package before him, and watched Eddy's eyes, he knew that he was listening to a murderer.

Eddy was not proud of the act, he was merely confident about it. He spoke of it as if it were a decision that he had made: "I'm going away. I won't be back." Not as if he had done something so horrible, so disgusting that hundreds of thousands of voices had been raised against him.

The women did not matter. It was not as if they were beautiful or intelligent. They were living on pennies in the streets, they had no souls, they were not of value. Even society said they were of no value.

It was *better* that he killed them, they would have died anyway. There was no return for them, they had no prospects, no hope.

And their faces were wrinkled and so sad, as though they were fleeing from something. They had no hearts, they said and did everything one way. It was all with a certain form, a certain gesture.

Eddy had known all about that. He had once slept with a prostitute who gave him the sores—James had never heard that story. They were not women, really. They were not really alive.

Their eyes were dead. They could laugh, they could sing, they spoke mostly in cockney, and they always had their hand out for those pennies.

They lifted their skirts and laughed, again standing up. Whatever comfort you wanted, they would give you. Except one.

That was what made Eddy do it. For that one comfort they would not give.

It was a comfort Eddy wanted more than anything in the world. That sense of overwhelming everything inside himself, until there was quiet, peace.

And the quiet did come finally as he walked back to the train station, as the sun came up and he approached St. James's Palace, as he knew that no power on earth could ever hurt him again.

He sat and ate his breakfast. He drank his morning tea. And there were traces of blood before his eyes, but the tea washed them away. He was a different person again, and *he had learned so much.*

As Eddy told his story to James, detailing the murders of Polly Nicholls and Annie Chapman, James's revulsion was overcome by a sense of amazement. Here was the future King of England admitting to him a deed that would have thrown the entire nation into a state of near-collapse. It was a calamity and yet Eddy conveyed his secret like someone announcing that he had stolen an item from a shop or that he had found the bloody contents of his package on the street outside the house.

James felt no fear for himself or for the royal personage who stood before him. The act itself was so improbable, so outrageous that he could barely react at all. Yet here it was, and if it were true, it was more than a phenomenon, it was an experience. How should he react? Should he share in it, or try to imagine it away as having never existed?

Eddy, the grandson of Queen Victoria, Eddy, who regarded him as his closest friend, Eddy, whom he had protected, nurtured, educated, was the murderer that all of London wanted to capture.

Just as his own ambition had once led him to dominate this young man and to become his intimate companion, he was once again moved to regard his crime as beneficial to himself. He, alone, knew the secret, and its knowledge gave him more power than he had ever imagined.

He sat for a long time before making any comment. There was still the question in his mind that he had imagined Eddy's story, that, in fact, it was entirely fictitious. But just as a response in him wished that it were not true, another part of him hoped it was.

On an autumn day in 1886, while out riding near Felixstowe, James Stephen had whipped his thoroughbred horse up a hill on which stood a windmill. As he reached the top of the rise, a sudden gust of wind startled the high-strung animal, backing it up into a descending vane of the windmill which smashed James across the skull.

James fell to the ground, unconscious, and remained that way for several hours before finally being discovered and given medical treatment. He never fully recovered. Through the months and years that followed, he experienced terrible headaches and involuntary lapses when events and places became indistinct. His father, a prominent judge, managed to obtain for him an appointment as Clerk Assize for the South Wales Circuit, but James was never able to fulfill his post. It was impossible for him to concentrate on any of his duties as he spent much of his time at home on an extended leave of absence.

The headaches grew worse and at times he imagined things that did not exist. Yet he was not sure afterward if he had heard them, seen them, or if his mind were playing tricks again.

Eddy's story had filled him with dread for himself. He was aware that the unreality and the real were somehow merging inside him, that he soon would not be able to distinguish between the two.

It was maddening to see things both ways, as real and unreal at the same time, as illusion, fantasy, self-deception, and then afterward wonder what he felt, what he really knew to be certain.

There had long been insanity in his family, and it was inevitable that he should inherit some of it. But it made him unhappy because that one choice had been removed, and he suddenly could not differentiate between his dreams and the world of reality which he knew must exist somewhere beyond the edge of his perception.

Eddy was real, had seemed real, and was now completely unreal. He was a murderer, no longer a prince, he roamed through Whitechapel destroying whores. It was inconceivable, ludicrous, yet James, himself, felt that he should join in.

He had read everything to do with the Whitechapel murders. A police official had now ordered that the eyes of Annie Chapman be photographed in the belief that the retinas might contain the image of her killer. This was obviously prompted by an article James had read that past winter in the *British Journal of Photography* about an assassin having been convicted in France on the strength of eyeball photography. It was not a new idea, but the police were obviously desperate to try anything.

They had collected a jumble of hearsay facts, generalized notions, and vague descriptions which led them to suppose that the murderer was a Jewish butcher, preferably foreign-born, with cruel eyes and the manner of a cat. There was one descriptive paragraph in the *Star* which, when James read it, especially amused him:

> A nameless reprobate—half beast, half man—is at large . . . Hideous malice, deadly cunning, insatiable thirst for blood—all these are the marks of the mad homicide. The ghoul-like creature, stalking down his victim like a Pawnee Indian, is simply drunk with blood, and he will have more.

In the September 27 issue of the *Lancet*, Police Surgeon Dr. George Bagster Phillips commented:

> The work was that of an expert, at least one who had such knowledge of anatomical or pathological examinations.

61

At this point, James felt that it was time to add something himself to the furor—a bit more notoriety, that he could control with his pen.

He would use red ink to make it instantly recognizable. He laughed as he addressed the letter to the Central News Agency on Fleet Street:

> Dear Boss,
>
> I keep on hearing the police have caught me, but they won't fix me just yet. I have laughed when they look so clever and talk about being on the right track. The joke about leather apron gave me real fits.
>
> I am down on whores and I shan't quit ripping them till I do get buckled. Grand work, the last job was. I gave the lady no time to squeal. How can they catch me now? I love my work and want to start again. You will soon hear of me and my funny little games.
>
> I saved some of the proper red stuff in a ginger beer bottle over the last job, to write with, but it went thick like glue and I can't use it. Red ink is fit enough, I hope. Ha! Ha!
>
> The next job I do I shall clip the lady's ears off and send them to the police, just for jolly, wouldn't you? Keep this letter back until I do a bit more work, then give it out straight. My knife's so nice and sharp, I want to get to work right away if I get a chance. Good luck,
>
> Yours truly,

How should he sign it? He needed a name that could be connected with the past. Scores of famous criminals came to mind—Jack Shepphard, Spring-Heeled Jack, Three-Fingered Jack, Slippery Jack . . .

He signed the letter and then added a comment:

> Don't mind me giving the trade name. Wasn't good enough to post this before I got all the red ink off my hands; curse it. No luck yet. They say I'm a doctor now. Ha! Ha!

Before he sent the letter, James showed it to Eddy. Eddy read it carefully, but made no comment. The weekend was approaching and James knew what was on Eddy's mind. He only worked on the weekend.

But James decided that he would not be there to see. He would leave the city. On September 30 he mailed a postcard to the Central News Agency. It outlined Eddy's plan:

You'll hear about Saucy Jack's work tomorrow. Double event this time. Number one squealed a bit; couldn't finish straight off. Had no time to get ears for police. Thanks for keeping last letter back till I go to work again.

To the bottom of the card, James added his own red ink-stained thumbprint. He signed it:

Jack the Ripper.

Chapter 5

THE FRENZY

A *Daily Telegraph* editorial, appearing shortly after Annie Chapman's murder, set the stage for the blood bath that was to come:

> Some mention was made at the inquest upon Annie Chapman of a wild proposal to photograph her glazed eyes, and so try if the dying retina would present any image of the cruel monster who killed her and mutilated her. Better have listened with ear of imagination at her poor swollen lips, for, without much fancy, a Home Secretary or Chairman of the Metropolitan Board of Works might have heard them murmuring:
>
> "We, your murdered sisters, are what the dreadful homes where we live have made us. Behind your fine squares and handsome streets you continue to leave our wild-beastlairs unchanged and uncleansed. The slums kill us, body and soul, with filth and shame and spread fever and death among your gentry also, while they are spawning beds for crime and social discontent. When it is possible for the poor of London to live and sleep in decency you will not pick up from backyards so many corpses like mine."

A relentless social reformer named Dr. Thomas J. Barnardo had dedicated his whole existence to rescuing children from the bitter squalor of Spitalfields. He was not alone in his efforts. The Reverend Andrew Mearns also roamed the streets and his observations were depressing.

> The child misery that one beholds is the most heart rending and appalling element in these discoveries; and of this not the least is the misery inherited from the vice of drunken and dissolute parents, and manifest in the stunted, misshapen, and often loathsome objects that we constantly meet in these localities. From the beginning of their lives they are utterly neglected; their bodies and rags are alive with vermin; they are subjected to the most cruel treatment; many of them have never seen a green field, and do not know what it is to go beyond the streets immediately around them, and they often pass the whole day without a morsel of food. Here is one of three years old picking up some dirty pieces of bread and eating them. We go in at the doorway where it is standing and find a little girl twelve years old. "Where is your mother?" "In the madhouse." "How long has she been there?" "Fifteen months." "Who looks after you?" The child, who is sitting at an old table making match-boxes, replies, "I look after my little brothers and sisters as well as I can."

Dr. Barnardo had founded a home for these waifs, gaining him much notoriety and the appellation: "Father of Nobody's Children."

Shortly after Annie Chapman's murder, he entered a doss house kitchen at 32 Flower-and-Dean Street where he saw several female residents sitting around a large open fire. They were discussing the murders and were obviously distraught at the fact that the only persons killed had been members of their class. Dr. Barnardo recalled that "they seemed thoroughly frightened at the dangers to which they were exposed."

To the right of the fire sat a big rawboned woman, with a hoarse Swedish accent, in her mid-forties. Her body seemed gaunt and underfed and she obviously had been drinking. For years afterward, Dr. Barnardo would recall the bitterness in her voice and her look of tense despair. "No one cares what becomes of us," she muttered to him. "Perhaps one of us will be killed next." Later, Dr. Barnardo would learn her name: Elizabeth Stride.

Her husband, John Thomas Stride, had drowned in the *Princess Alice* disaster with two of their nine children. She had escaped only by climbing up a rope and hanging there as the vessel was sinking. She had watched her youngest child die in her husband's arms. These and other details of that great ship disaster were re-created over and over by Liz Stride for the benefit of her sisters-in-trade who roamed the boulevards of Whitechapel.

In the Thames police court, where she frequently faced charges of being drunken and disorderly, she would let out a cry of shrill indignation, claiming that she never touched liquor at all, but was subject to spells of fainting and morning sickness. Suddenly she would fall to the floor and begin to twitch and make fierce pitiful cries that prompted the police readily to release her.

Liz Stride played many roles.

Her maiden name was Elisabeth Gustaafsdotter. She had been born near Göteborg, Sweden, on November 27, 1843. This would have meant that she had her nine children by the time she was twenty-five, as the *Princess Alice* was run down and sunk by a collier on September 3, 1878.

More probably the great myth with which she surrounded her life was concocted from the fact that her husband, John Stride, was a joiner who helped to build ships and although he was twice her age she married him to escape domestic servitude. The tale of her nine children, which she said she bore prior to 1878, was also a face-saving concoction. Neither she nor John Stride ever had any children.

Elizabeth Stride was last seen alive by Police Constable William Smith at twelve thirty-five Sunday morning, September 30. She was standing on Berner Street just south of Commercial Road, speaking to a man of medium height, about twenty-eight years of age, clean-shaven, and of respectable appearance. He wore a dark overcoat, a hard felt deerstalker hat, and was carrying a newspaper parcel about eight inches in length.

Major Henry Smith, Acting Police Commissioner for the City of London, was obsessed by the identity of the killer. As he pored over the dispatches that hourly arrived at Scotland Yard, he formulated a strategy as to how the investigation should be handled. Especially intriguing was the letter in red ink which the Central News Agency on Fleet Street had received signed "Jack the Ripper." It was obvious to him that the killer was an insane exhibitionist who derived tremendous delight from flaunting his deeds in the face of a police force which now seemed incapable of apprehending him.

Unfortunately Major Smith was powerless as well. Neither of the two murders had been committed in that mile-square area designated as the City, which was under his supervision.

He could not cross over into Whitechapel, as this would have resulted in an immediate blast from Metropolitan Police Commissioner Charles Warren. But it was obvious to Major Smith that neither Warren nor his staff was competent to handle the situation. They were ex-soldiers, not policemen. And certainly none of them were detectives.

While arrests and suspects flooded station houses in the East End, Major Smith quietly sent his officers out into the streets to make inquiries. His men interviewed every butcher doing business in the area and he also put two dozen or so more into plainclothes to mingle in shops, stores, and pubs and to keep their ears open. It was not the prescribed way to investigate a case, and Major Smith knew that he could be criticized for his actions should they be found out, but he proceeded in the belief that any detail or thread of information might prove vital in uncovering the murderer's identity. "It was subversive of discipline," he reported later, "but I had my men well supervised by senior officers. The weather was lovely and I have little doubt that they thoroughly enjoyed themselves sitting on doorsteps smoking their pipes, hanging about public houses, and gossiping with all and sundry."

Major Smith also issued orders that every man and woman seen after midmight within the precincts of the City should be identified and followed to their destination. But on the morning of September 30, there occurred an ironic series of events which not only thwarted his precautions but also frustrated the one chance he would have to encounter his elusive prey.

At 8 P.M. on the evening of September 29, a woman wearing a green dress imprinted with daisies and yellow lilies and a thin cloth jacket with an imitation fur collar was arrested for being drunk and disorderly. She was taken to Bishopsgate Station in the City, where she identified herself as Catherine Eddowes.

She was a tiny woman who had run away with a soldier, Thomas Conway, when she was nineteen. His initials were still tattooed on her forearm. She had borne Conway's three children during the twelve years they had lived together. They finally parted without ever marrying.

She now lived with a market porter, John Kelly. At the beginning of September, she and Kelly had gone hop-picking near Maidstone in Kent, in order to earn a few shillings. They had returned to London on September 27, with prospects of sudden wealth. Catherine Eddowes believed she knew the identity of the Whitechapel murderer.

She felt certain that she would be able to obtain the reward money for the killer's capture. "I'm sure I know who he is," she had confided to Kelly.

After their arrival in London, both she and Kelly got drunk on cheap gin and took a night's lodging at No. 55 Flower-and-Dean Street. The next day they were completely out of money and Kelly had to pawn his shoes for half a crown. He stood outside the pawnshop in his bare feet while Catherine went inside and made the arrangement. Leaving the pawnshop, they spent the money on more gin.

Finally, on September 29, after searching unsuccessfully for odd jobs, they parted company. Catherine told Kelly that she was going to Bermondsey to borrow money from her daughter, Annie, who was married to a lampblack packer. As she left Kelly, he called after her, "Watch out for the Ripper." "Don't worry about me," Catherine answered, "I can take care of myself."

Shortly after midnight on the morning of September 30, Catherine Eddowes awakened in jail from a drunken stupor and began singing to herself. She then demanded to be released. "As soon as you are able to take care of yourself," the jailer told her. A half hour later she seemed completely sober and the jailer in charge, realizing that it was too late for her to buy more drink, agreed to release her. Contrary to Major Smith's orders, she was not followed from the stationhouse, but wandered away, alone, down Houndsditch.

Berner Street led into a narrow courtyard that was almost pitch black. On one side of the courtyard was the meeting center for a group of immigrant Russian, German, and Polish Jews, known as the International Workmen's Educational Club. Directly opposite, on the other side of the yard, stood a row of cottages inhabited by sweatshop tailors and cigarette makers. A high wall closed off the end of the courtyard while a pair of large wooden gates stood at the entrance leading into Berner Street. The courtyard was unlighted and the residents in the row of cottages had long since retired. It was almost 1 A.M.

When Eddy was noticed by Police Constable William Smith talking to the woman he had picked up a few moments before, he instinctively tried to ease the newspaper-encased knife closer to his body. The officer, who was alone, gazed for a moment at the newspaper-wrapped package but did not stop. Out of the corner of his eye, Eddy watched as the blue form continued down toward the railroad yards.

It was a wet rainy night and Eddy was already soaked to the skin. A slight wind was blowing from the east, causing him to shiver a little as he stood waiting for the right moment. He did not want to be disturbed.

The pubs were all closed and there were only a few spotted lights from a nearby building where several voices were raised in occasional muffled conversation. The people inside the building did not seem to be speaking English; at least Eddy could not make out what they were saying. It did not worry him, however, as the building's entrance was in darkness and the front door was shut.

The narrow courtyard that lay beyond was deserted. Eddy slipped a few pennies into the woman's hand. There was already something in it, a small bag of perfumed breath pastils. She was Swedish. Once or twice she muttered a little phrase which Eddy could not understand. But there was no question that she was drunk. She was a big woman, very tall and thin. She wore a flower in her jacket and a silk scarf knotted about her neck. He could barely see her eyes in the darkness as he slowly led her through the wooden gates into the courtyard.

Beyond the gates was a shrouded patch of total black hidden just behind the adjoining walls. Here Eddy stopped as she reached up and tugged playfully at the red bandanna he wore around his neck. At that moment, he let the newspaper fall from the knife.

He did it with a slight movement and then hesitated. In her wavering, unsteady daze, she noticed nothing. He reached up with his hand, feeling for her scarf, then tugged her slowly downward to her knees. Suddenly he gave her scarf a quick yank as he swung the knife across his hip, cutting through her throat.

She fell backward to the curb and for a second he could not see her body in the darkness. He bent down, holding the knife upraised at the handle. At that moment he heard a horse's hooves coming toward him in the darkness.

Eddy stood up in alarm. Glancing around the courtyard, he saw that there was no escape except through the wooden entrance gates. He tore through them as he heard the sound of the horse's hooves clopping closer from the direction of the railroad yards. Racing up Berner Street, he hurriedly tried to bury the knife inside his coat.

The clock of St. Mary's Whitechapel struck one. The steward's pony clopped slowly, painfully along the cobblestones toward the International Workmen's Educational Club. Louis Diemshutz had suffered through a trying day of hawking cheap jewelry from the back of his cart in front of the Crystal Palace in Sydenham. His conglomeration of imitation ruby and topaz brooches, ten-shilling music boxes, cameos, tea trays, and mother-of-pearl shirt studs, had drawn few customers.

Yet he still had more work to do. The members of the International Workmen's Educational Club would expect him to close up after their open-house activities, which included their usual Saturday night debate. Their subject for that evening had been "The Necessity for Socialism Among Jews." As he turned into the narrow courtyard off Berner Street, he noticed that a few lights in the building were still burning.

Half-asleep, he wished he were already home in bed. Suddenly his pony stopped dead, and then with a jerk began to back away from something in the darkness just inside the gate. Diemshutz was all but thrown off the cart.

He leaped to the ground, patted the pony's nose, and, taking his whip groped in the pitch-black area along the wall.

He felt something soft. When he struck a match, he saw that it was the body of a woman.

Diemshutz did not stop. Rushing through the front door of the clubhouse, he encountered Zozebrodski, one of the members. Zozebrodski hurriedly returned with him to the spot. Both men lit a candle and bent down to peer at the woman's dark form.

She was lying on her left side with her legs drawn up as if she had been buckled in half. Her clothes were wet from the rain. A dark bloody trickle dripped slowly from her neck onto the ground.

Diemshutz cautiously touched her body. It was still warm. She had been dead barely more than a few minutes. At that second, a terrible realization struck him. He had barely missed surprising the killer.

Eddy continued up Commercial Road, pulling his cap down tighter because of the wind. He had to move more slowly now because of the knife inside his coat. He felt no fear.

Indeed, the horse's hooves coming toward him and his escape from the courtyard filled him with a sense of glee. It was as if all the world were suddenly converging on him, yet he managed to escape, to be freer than he had ever been.

How could anyone catch him? He had always dreamed of being invisible, and perhaps now he was. He could continue to escape, and each time they might look but he would be gone. Yet he worried a little about the policeman. He had noticed the newspaper-wrapped knife under his arm. That policeman would remember.

But it was not Eddy that he had passed talking to a woman on Berner Street. It was a stranger in a dark coat and a deerstalker. There was no way he could link the two. Eddy was free. Once again, he had escaped.

Eddy turned down Aldgate. He walked casually now, quietly. The street was empty. He passed the Aldgate underground station, into Houndsditch, then stopped.

Coming toward him was a woman in a black bonnet. She was small, thin, and alone. Eddy waited for her at the end of the street.

Joseph Lawende and his two friends had been at the Imperial Club all evening. When they left at 1:30 P.M., they sauntered up Duke's Place past Creechurch Lane. A woman's laughter caused them to turn as they passed the entrance to Mitre Square.

Lawende saw a young man, about thirty, with a small, fair moustache, dressed in a navy serge with a deerstalker's cap talking to a small, thin woman in a black bonnet. The man was wearing a red bandanna around his neck.

Mitre Square was dark and empty, with a wooden fence at one end and the Kearley and Tonge Warehouse at the other. Lawende and his companions continued up Duke's Place, talking among themselves.

At the same moment, Police Constable Edward Watkins was making his rounds along Leadenhall Street, one block away. He had turned, as he did each evening, up Gracechurch Street into Bishopsgate and then along Leadenhall Street, back into Mitre Square.

As Eddy spoke quietly to the woman, he beckoned for her to follow him into the square. The passageway led along a wooden fence. At the end was a gate and a building with a steel-grated window. There was no light from the building.

Eddy suddenly pulled the woman closer to him, as he moved quickly into the shadows. At that second, she pulled away. She

The Prince of Wales, Princess Alexandra, and the future Jack the Ripper. *Culver Pictures*

Alexandra and her beloved Georgie. *Culver Pictures*

Sandringham.

The back alley behind a row of doss houses in Spitalfields.

The coal-burning cut-and-cover railway on which Eddy escaped from Whitechapel following Polly Nicholls' murder.

Goulston Street on a Sunday morning a short distance from the wall with its chalk message: "The Juwes are not the men that will be blamed for nothing."

Prostitutes in white aprons wait along Dorset Street a few feet from the entrance to Miller's Court.

Three photographs of Eddy which show his rapid deterioration between June 1890 and August 1891. Left, Eddy and his betrothed, May of Teck (who later became Queen Mary). *Radio Times Hulton Picture Library*

Eddy's lover; James Stephen.

At the top of the page is James's signature (JK Stephen). Below it is the letter he wrote to George Lusk, Chairman of the Whitechapel Vigilance Committee. By changing the angle of the paper in order to form upright letters, he attempted not only to disguise his handwriting, but purposely misspelled and ran together such words as "kidne," "t other," "wate," and "Mishter." A similarity is noted between the "K" in his signature and the "k" ending the final word, "Lusk." But more revealing is the word "whil," ending the second to last line of the message, as compared with his signature.

Lord Salisbury. *Radio Times Hulton Picture Library*

had noticed the long object which he held, gripped beneath his coat.

She turned, and with a jerk pulled free. He caught the back of her coat collar. She let out a squeal as he threw her against the building wall. He had her by the neck now, and as she squirmed, he smashed her face-first into the wall again and again, until he felt the bones in her nose crack. He quickly yanked her back onto the sidewalk and bent down over her.

Slitting her throat with the knife, he then ripped the knife downward through her body, tearing her clothes back, pulling out her organs, thrusting them over her shoulder. Then he sliced off one of her kidneys and held it in the folds of her dress. He cut off the lower part of her dress, clutching the piece of her kidney between it.

Her eyes were closed. Her body twitched uncontrollably. He slit the lids of her eyes until they opened. He stood up, still clutching the section of her dress. Then he turned and hurried back up the passageway.

A moment later, Police Constable Edward Watkins entered Mitre Square from St. James's Passage. He flashed his bull's-eye lantern along the wooden fence, the gate, and the adjoining steel-grated window of the building in the southwest corner. Suddenly his light illumined a body and woman's clothing. Drawing closer, he shivered as he saw the pool of blood surrounding her. She was lying on her back; at least, what remained of her. She had been ripped apart, as he later related, "like a pig in a market," with her face smashed in and her entrails thrust in a heap around her neck.

The frightened policeman tore across the courtyard to the Kearley and Tonge Warehouse. The door was slightly ajar, and he screamed to the nightwatchman who was sweeping the stairs, "For God's sake, help me—there's a woman—" He tremblingly gestured toward the other end of the courtyard. "She's been cut to pieces."

Eddy ran across Houndsditch right into the series of connecting alleys from Harrow Place to Middlesex Street. He stopped a second to catch his breath. There was blood all over his hands and the front of his coat. He managed to conceal the knife in the section of the woman's dress he had cut from the body.

He had to rid himself of the blood, to wash it off somehow.

He crouched in the darkness for a long moment, and then raced across Middlesex into another alley between two rows of buildings. He hated the blood all over him. He had to get it off before it began to dry. At the end of the alley, just off Goulston Street, was a passageway leading to a staircase.

He quickly tore the piece of dress in half and wiped the blood from the front of his coat. As he stood there in the darkness, he noticed something very small and white at the foot of the staircase. He bent over and discovered that it was a piece of chalk.

At that moment he thought of James. If James had been there, he might have written something on the wall, some note to further confuse those persons who doted on such details.

But James was not there. So Eddy could only smile as he wrote what he imagined James might have written. He even misspelled the word "Jews" so that no one would mistake that it was the same person who had written that amusing little letter to the Central News Agency in Fleet Street.

Seconds away, Major Henry Smith's hansom sped toward Mitre Square. Accompanying the Acting Police Commissioner was a two-hundred-pound police Superintendent and three detectives hanging from behind.

The Major had been tossing in his bed, trying to sleep at the Cloak Lane Police Station not far from Southwark Bridge, when, shortly before 2 A.M., the bell at his head began ringing violently. "What is it?" he roared irritably through the tube. "Another murder, sir," came the reply. "This time in the City—in Mitre Square."

There was a noisy railway depot at the entrance to the police station and a furrier's warehouse behind, which meant that the rancid smell of skins had made Major Smith nauseated. He was half-awake now, in a terrible mood, when the bell ringing above his head came as a welcome relief. He jumped out of bed, dressed in no time, and made for the street.

Cannon, Monument, Gracechurch, Major Smith counted each

74

minute. Finally his hansom tore around the corner of Leadenhall Street into Mitre Square. The Major leaped off and headed toward the crowd of police officers huddling around the body. She lay on her back, her left leg extended, her right leg bent. As the Major drew closer, he saw that her throat had been slit and her body horribly mutilated.

Her dress, which was imprinted with daisies and golden lilies, had been pushed up to her waist, revealing a faded linsey skirt, a dark green alpaca petticoat, and a soiled white chemise. On her feet she wore brown ribbed knee stockings and a pair of men's laced boots. Her black cloth jacket had an imitation fur collar and three large metal buttons. A black straw bonnet, trimmed with black beads and green and black velvet, was still tied to her head with a ribbon.

Searching her pockets, the Major found a white handkerchief with a red border, a matchbox containing cotton, a blunt table knife with a white bone handle, two short clay pipes, a red cigarette case, a printed handbill, five pieces of soap, a small tin box containing tea and sugar, a broken pair of spectacles, a three-cornered checked handkerchief, a small comb, one red mitten, and a ball of worsted yarn. It was then that the Major was told that her name was Catherine Eddowes, that she had been arrested earlier that evening for being drunk and disorderly, but had been released from Bishopsgate police station at shortly after 1 A.M.

Major Smith was furious. If she had been followed, as he had ordered, he now would have the murderer in custody. But his orders had not been obeyed. As he stared down at the body, he wished that it might not end this way, that he might be left with some lead to the murderer's identity.

In a matter of seconds, Major Smith's wish was granted. Police Constable Alfred Long, H Division, Whitechapel, had been passing the Peabody dwellings in Goulston Street when he spotted a bloodstained rag which turned out to be part of a woman's clothing. It was lying in a passageway leading to the staircase of Nos. 118 and 119. On the wall, directly above the bloody fragment, was a message written in white chalk:

The Juwes are not the men that will be blamed for nothing.

Meanwhile, the courtyard off Berner Street was in an uproar. Police constables from H Division, Whitechapel, had shut the two wooden gates to keep out the thrill seekers as they began interrogating the steward, Diemshutz, and the twenty or so Russian and Polish members of the International Workmen's Educational Club. The members' hands and clothing were examined for bloodstains, their names and addresses were recorded, but when the police began to ransack their clubhouse, they rose up in fury. To add to the unrest, few of them could speak any English.

Another cordon of police questioned the tenants—the sweatshop tailors and cigarette makers—who lived in the row of cottages on the opposite side of the courtyard. None of them could remember hearing any outcries or sounds of violence.

William West, a printer residing at 40 Berner Street, had crossed the courtyard at 12:30 A.M. and had noticed the gates were open, but was certain that the courtyard was deserted. Morris Eagle, a club member, had crossed the courtyard at 12:40 A.M., but saw nothing unusual.

Joseph Lave, who had passed through the yard at about ten minutes to one, stated: "The court was very dark, and so I had to grope my way along the right-hand wall (*where the body was discovered*). I would have stumbled over the body if it had been there at the time."

Police Surgeon Dr. George Bagster Phillips established the victim's identity as Elizabeth Stride, also known as "Long Liz," a forty-five-year-old widow of Swedish birth. Her death had been caused by hemorrhage resulting from a knife severing her windpipe and left carotid artery.

The crowd which now gathered in Berner Street numbered over sixty. They became suddenly silent as the two wooden gates opened and Elizabeth Stride's canvas-draped corpse was slowly wheeled toward them.

After Eddy had left the passageway, he kept to the back alleys, heading north on Goulston Street toward Spitalfields Market. He crossed Artillery Lane into Dorset and then spotted what he had been hoping for. Set back about six yards from the street was a public sink.

Bending over the sink, he washed the blood from his hands and the front of his coat. The street was still deserted but he would have to cut through Spitalfields Market or turn eastward and cross Commercial Street to Brick Lane and back into Whitechapel. If he headed west and circled down Bishopsgate, he could catch the train at Liverpool Street Station.

It was 2:30 A.M. The first train would not leave until after five. He could hide in the station but the police would be looking for him. It would be better if he kept moving westward through the back streets. On foot, he would be home in less than an hour.

Major Smith arrived at the staircase just off Goulston Street and identified the torn piece of clothing as part of the dress belonging to Catherine Eddowes. He stationed Detectives Hunt and Halse on the scene to photograph the chalk writing on the wall as soon as it was daylight. He then proceeded to trace the killer's path northward.

The fact that the murderer had stopped to write his message on the wall, which was discovered by Police Constable Alfred Long, H Division, at 2:55 A.M., meant that he was no more than minutes ahead of him. Also, the fact that he must certainly have blood on his clothes and person would make him easily identifiable.

As Major Smith hurried along Goulston Street, he saw one of his constables running toward him. The panting constable, between breaths, managed to convey that he had just discovered fresh blood near a public sink off Dorset Street.

Smith felt confident now as he raced up Goulston Street. He was very close.

Arriving at Dorset Street, he quickly examined the sink which was set back slightly from the street. Not quite all of the blood-stained water had gurgled down the drain. But which way had the murderer run?

Major Smith hesitated a moment before deciding. The killer

would be heading home—and since he knew the area so thoroughly, that could only be Whitechapel.

Sir Charles Warren waited in the darkness off Cleveland Row until Eddy arrived at the entrance to Marlborough House. It was almost 4 A.M.

The Prince was wearing a blue serge jacket with a felt deerstalker, and a red bandanna around his neck. There was no doubt in Charles Warren's mind that the young man he was observing was the Whitechapel murderer.

At first, he had scoffed at the possibility. A policeman had seen Eddy, on the morning following the Chapman murder, arrive at the royal residence at 5 A.M. carrying a newspaper-wrapped package. Warren had laughed at the officer's suspicions, but afterward, on his own, had tracked the Prince's movements, and from an informant in the Palace had learned that the Prince had also arrived home in the early morning hours following the Nicholls' murder in Buck's Row.

Now there was no question.

His one course of action was to protect the Royal Family at any cost. It was his duty to the Queen that no one should suspect her grandson. And Charles Warren, perhaps more than any other government official in England, recognized where his duty lay.*

By 5 A.M., Warren arrived on the scene at Goulston Street. There he encountered Detectives Halse and Hunt, who had been left to photograph the chalk-written message on the wall. Warren informed the two officers that he did not want the writing photographed. He then ordered them to rub out the words completely.

Major Smith's Inspector, James MacWilliams, who was also on the scene, argued that it would soon be daylight and that it would be a grave error to destroy such evidence, as it could provide a valuable clue to the killer's identity. But Warren would not listen.

---

* In a memorandum to Home Secretary Matthews (now part of the Home Office File), Commissioner Warren pointed out that the Ripper murders were "exceptional" in nature and had to be handled in "a very special way." In this same memorandum he also implied that the murderer would never be brought to justice.

Goulston Street was beginning to fill with peddlers setting up stalls for the regular Sunday morning open-air market along Petticoat Lane. His decision, he explained, was made on the basis that the message might lead to anti-Jewish rioting.

Detective Halse offered a compromise. Perhaps the message might be temporarily covered up, or perhaps they might rub out the top line, or just the word "Juwes." But Warren was adamant. Finally, he took a sponge and rubbed out the words himself.

Chapter 6

THE OUTCRY

Within minutes Major Smith arrived at Nos. 118 and 119 Goulston Street fuming with frustration. He had attempted to track the killer through the back alleys off Brick Lane, down and across Heneage Street, Chicksand Street, Old Montague Street, and finally into Whitechapel Road, but his efforts had proven futile. Either the Ripper had chosen a different escape route, northward toward Bethnal Green, then across Shoreditch, or else he had simply vanished into thin air.

In desperation, the Major had penetrated deeply into Metropolitan Police territory, threatening a jurisdictional dispute, but there was no turning back. He visited half a dozen police stations in the hope that a suspect might have been picked up who would turn out to be the murderer. But once again, he was disappointed.

Finally, back at the entrance to the passageway off Goulston Street, he suffered his greatest setback of the morning. The chalk-written message on the wall was gone. He flew into a blind rage when Inspector MacWilliams described how Sir Charles Warren had personally rubbed out the words before they could be photographed. "It was an unpardonable blunder," Major Smith related afterward. Bitterly he added: "The writing on the wall may have been written—and, I think, probably was written—to throw the police off the scent, to divert suspicion from the Gentiles and throw it upon the Jews. It may have been written by the murderer, or it may not. To obliterate the words that might have given us a most valuable clue, more especially after I had sent a man to stand over them till they were photographed, was not only indiscreet, but unwarrantable."

It was a small consolation to Major Smith when later that day Sir Robert Anderson, the new head of CID, described Warren's erasure of the writing on the wall as "an act of crass stupidity." Anderson, however, failed to name Warren as the one responsible. "It was done by the officers of the uniformed force in the division upon an order issued by one of my colleagues," Anderson explained. But the "colleague's" name was not disclosed.

Anderson's own absence from the murder investigation was noted by the *Pall Mall Gazette*:

> You may seek Dr. Anderson in Scotland Yard, you may look for him in Whitehall-place, but you will not find him. Dr. Anderson, with all the arduous duties of his office still to learn, is preparing himself for his apprenticeship by taking a pleasant holiday in Switzerland!

To avoid further repercussions, Anderson was forced to hurry back to London from his vacation in Switzerland on the afternoon following the two murders. The next morning he met with Henry Matthews, the Home Secretary, and Sir Charles Warren. Matthews told Anderson that from that point on they would hold *him* responsible for tracking down the murderer.

Anderson declined the responsibility, shaking his head. "I hold myself responsible," he replied, "to take all *legitimate* means to find him." His first planned counteroffensive was to warn all prostitutes roaming the streets after midnight that the police would not protect them. Warren agreed to back him up. He would assign seven top police officials full time to the Ripper investigation with instructions to position every available man throughout the alleys and streets of the East End to try to catch the killer red-handed. A house-to-house hunt would be conducted in Spitalfields and ten thousand handbills would be printed urging anyone who knew "any person to whom suspicion might be attached" to communicate immediately with the nearest police.

No police officer would be allowed to give interviews to the press. This policy was Warren's most emphatic method of keeping a net of secrecy surrounding the investigation. He argued that newspapers provided no help at all and quite often were a hindrance. Both Anderson and Matthews agreed. Secrecy was now their most effective ally.

Later that day, the Home Office officially announced that no reward would be offered for the killer's capture. The decision was based on the contention that offering a reward would too strongly tempt vigilantes to form Blood Money conspiracies. The announcement was attacked by the Lord Mayor of London. On behalf of the City Corporation, he offered a £500 reward for "such information as shall lead to the discovery and conviction of the murderer or murderers." Various organizations then stepped forward to add to the reward. The Tower Hamlets battalion of the Royal Engineers not only offered an additional £100, but volunteered fifty men "either for the protection of the public or for finding out the criminals."

Aroused citizens demanded that the government take the lead. Several donors, employing the *Financial News* as their transactor, forwarded bequests totaling £300 to Matthews, pleading with him to offer the money "in the name of the government."

The sums were returned the following day with a note from Matthews' secretary to the editor of the *Financial News*:

> I am directed to thank you, and the gentlemen whose names you forwarded, for the liberality of their offer, which Mr. Matthews much regrets he is unable to accept.

Thus, the citizenry and the press were held at arm's length as Sir Charles Warren and his two associates proceeded with their own private investigation. But Warren's methods had not deceived everyone. A crowd of a thousand people met in Victoria Park to pass a resolution demanding that both he and Matthews resign and make way for men who would leave no stone unturned to find the murderer.

Even more dramatically, a wild-looking Irishman named Michael Kidney, who had been living on and off with Elizabeth Stride just prior to her death, staggered drunkenly into the Leman Street Police Station a few moments after he identified her body at St. George's mortuary. His clothes were torn and his face was scratched and bruised as if he had been beaten in the streets. Grabbing the desk sergeant by the lapel, he shouted, "If Liz Stride had been murdered on my beat, I'd bloody well go out and shoot myself!"

Returning from an open-air meeting on Plumstead Common, music critic George Bernard Shaw noted: "All the talk on the train was about the two murders." Shaw promptly penned a letter to the *Star*, in which he leveled a wry broadside at the upper-crust establishment's pretense in helping the poor:

> If the habits of Duchesses only admitted of their being decoyed into Whitechapel backyards, a single experiment in slaughterhouse anatomy on an aristocratic victim might fetch in a round half million and save the necessity of sacrificing four women of the people.

Comparing the efforts of the socialist movement, for which he was an ardent spokesman, to the methods of the murderer, he acidly observed:

> Whilst we conventional Social Democrats were wasting our time on education, agitation and organization, some independent genius has taken the matter in hand, and by simply murdering and disembowelling four women, converted the proprietary press to an inept sort of communism.

The *Star* added in an editorial of its own:

> There is the off-chance—too horrible to contemplate—that we have a social experimentation abroad determined to make the classes see and feel how the masses live.

Instinctively, both George Bernard Shaw and the *Star* editors had touched on the truth. If they only could have penetrated the social issue, and perhaps have sensed the more human problem, that of the wretched, the neglected, the inhumanly treated pitted against the hypocrisy of a social structure that would not open its heart, they might have envisioned Eddy's motives. The actions of "the Ripper," as he was forever to be known, were prompted by an urge to *cry out* to some infinite source of understanding. "Sexual murders are the most difficult of all for police to bring home to the perpetrators," wrote Sir Melville Macnaghten, a highly regarded London Police Commissioner two generations later, "for motives there are none; only a lust for blood, and in many cases a hatred of woman as woman."

But it was James who hated women, not Eddy. It was James who had signed the letter "Jack the Ripper."

Mitre Square had become a tourist attraction. Crowds of thrill seekers swarmed in and out along Mitre Street, Creechurch Lane, and St. James's Passage, to peer at the spot where Catherine Eddowes' body had lain. Hardly had the blood dried when a baby belonging to one of the women in the throng began to cry. Its mother held up the infant: "Does it want to see the blood, bless its heart? So it shall. Take a good look at it, my pet. You may see enough of it if this sort of thing keeps up." It was reported that the child immediately quieted down. In Berner Street a street hawker made a quick profit selling swordsticks with the cry: "Here you are, sixpence for a swordstick—just the sort to do 'em in."

Terror was mounting, and the threat of panic was intensified by the fact that no one knew the murderer's identity or could even describe his physical appearance. Most Londoners were convinced that there must be something unusual about him; he could not be a person such as themselves.

A *Star* reader, writing from the Isle of Wight, believed that he might be a large ape escaped from some wild beast show. Another theory was that the murderer had been horribly disfigured by venereal disease and was now avenging himself on the female sex. It was suggested that female dummies should be placed throughout Whitechapel in the darkest, most desolate spots and that in their arms and legs would be powerful springs "capable of being released by moderate force, such as raising the chin or pressing the throat. Once released, these springs would act like the arm of an *octopus* and hold the person entrapped, while a sound resembling a police whistle might proceed from the machine." Another suggestion was that women should wear velvet-covered steel collars or a soft collar with "fine sharp pointed stings that the infernal assassin will be thus hardly wounded . . . At the same moment the officer will turn round and take hold of the murderer above the hand, turning it with all the power of his two hands against the breast of the scoundrel; thus, that this monster must bore his own knife into his own breast." The five hundred or so additional detectives that might be employed to trap the killer in this way could be recruited from the young German Kaiser, who was obviously fond of Queen Victoria and would willingly loan her a thousand detectives from Berlin.

A final precaution was suggested: all detectives should pretend to be intoxicated, wear iron collars and thin body armor.

Fourteen hundred letters poured into Scotland Yard. But one letter, the most important one of all, was received by George Lusk, Chairman of the Whitechapel Vigilance Committee. The handwriting seemed more rushed and feverish than before and there were heavy ink blotches covering the page. It was accompanied by a cardboard box containing Catherine Eddowes' left kidney.

Mr. Lusk went immediately to Major Smith. There was no question in the Major's mind to whom the grisly piece of flesh belonged, but to be certain, he had it analyzed by Dr. Openshaw, the Pathological Curator of the London Hospital Museum. It was in an advanced state of Bright's disease, exactly as the one which had been left in Catherine Eddowes' body had been. As a final proof, attached to it was a one-inch section of venal artery (which is about three inches long). When the kidney had been severed, the killer had left two inches of venal artery still attached inside Catherine Eddowes' body. The letter accompanying it was written

85

in a perverse jargon which indicated to Major Smith the writer's building madness.

From hell

   Mr. Lusk
     Sir
     I send you half the kidne I took from one woman, prasarved it for you, tother piece I fried and ate it; was very nice. I may send you the bloody knif that took it out if you only wate whil longer.
     Signed   Catch me when
                          you can
                    Mister Lusk

A few days later George Lusk received a second note scribbled on a postcard:

     Say Boss, you seem rare frightened. Guess I like to give you fits, but can't stop long enough to let you box of toys play copper games with me, but hope to see you when I don't hurry too much. Goodbye, Boss.

The question of the murderer's expertise with a knife was explored during Catherine Eddowes' inquest held at Golden Lane mortuary. Once again, it was suspected that he might be a doctor, until Dr. Frederick Brown, who had performed the post-mortem, was questioned by City Solicitor Crawford.

MR. CRAWFORD: Does the nature of the wounds lead you to any conclusion as to the kind of instrument with which they were inflicted?

DR. BROWN: With a sharp knife, and it must have been pointed; and from the cut in the abdomen I should say the knife was at least six inches long.

MR. CRAWFORD: Would you consider that the person who inflicted the wounds possessed great anatomical skill?

DR. BROWN: A good deal of knowledge as to the position of the organs in the abdominal cavity and the way of removing them.

MR. CRAWFORD: Could the organs removed be used for any professional purpose?

DR. BROWN: They would be of no use for a professional purpose.

MR. CRAWFORD: You spoke of the extraction of the left kidney. Would it require great skill and knowledge to remove it?

DR. BROWN: It would require a great deal of knowledge as to its position to remove it. It is easily overlooked. It is covered by a membrane.

MR. CRAWFORD: Would not such a knowledge be likely to be possessed by one accustomed to cutting up animals?

DR. BROWN: Yes.

It was not considered by either the Police Surgeon or the City Solicitor that the murderer might have closely *observed* others who were expert at cutting up animals.

City Solicitor Crawford then tried to block Joseph Lawende's testimony. Lawende related that he had seen Catherine Eddowes talking to a man at the entrance to Mitre Square when he had passed by with his friends up Duke Street. This was minutes before her mutilated remains were discovered by Police Constable Watkins.

"What sort of man was he?" Coroner Langham asked. Before Lawende could reply, Crawford interrupted: "Unless the jury wish it, I have special reason why no description of this man should be given at this time." Lawende's description was never given, as obviously Charles Warren's hand was ever present. Somehow he had gotten to City Solicitor Crawford.

But Major Smith would not let the matter rest. He interrogated Lawende on his own. The description of the killer as supplied by Lawende was extremely accurate. The man he saw was about thirty years old (Eddy was twenty-five), five feet nine inches in height (Eddy was five feet eight), with a small fair moustache, dressed in something like a navy serge coat, with a deerstalker's cap. Major Smith immediately circulated the description throughout the City, adding one more detail that Lawende had provided: the killer wore a red neckerchief. To this information, Major Smith added his own comment: "It was bright moonlight, almost as light as day, and Lawende saw them distinctly. This was, without doubt, the murderer and his victim."

Sir Charles Warren was not able to interfere with Police Constable William Smith's giving his description of the killer at

Elizabeth Stride's inquest held at the Vestry Hall in Cable Street. Constable Smith was questioned by Coroner Wynne E. Baxter. Once again, his description fitted Eddy perfectly. He recounted how he had been passing along Berner Street at 12:30 A.M., when he saw the victim:

> CORONER BAXTER: Did you see the man who was talking to her?
> CONSTABLE SMITH: Yes, I noticed he had a newspaper parcel in his hand. It was about eight inches in length and six or eight inches in width. He was about five feet seven inches as near as I could say. He had on a hard felt deerstalker hat of dark color and dark clothes.
> CORONER BAXTER: What kind of a coat was it?
> CONSTABLE SMITH: An overcoat. He wore dark trousers.
> CORONER BAXTER: Can you give any idea as to his age?
> CONSTABLE SMITH: About twenty-eight years.
> CORONER BAXTER: Can you give any idea as to who he was?
> CONSTABLE SMITH: No sir, I cannot. He was of respectable appearance.

The *Police Gazette* printed the description, but, as was often the case with the press, diluted it with various inaccuracies and the description of a second witness, a laborer in an indigo warehouse named William Marshall, who insisted that he also had seen the killer talking to the victim at 11:45 P.M., *one hour and a half* prior to her murder.

> At 12:35 a.m. 30th September, with Elizabeth Stride found murdered on the same date in Berner Street at 1 a.m., a man, age 28, height 5 feet 8 inches, complexion dark, small dark moustache; dress, black diagonal coat, hard felt hat, collar and tie, respectable appearance, carried a parcel wrapped up in newspaper.

> At 12:45 a.m., 30th, with the same woman in Berner Street, a man, age about 30, height 5 feet 5 inches; complexion fair, hair dark, small brown moustache, full face, broad shoulders; dress, dark jacket and trousers, black cap with peak.

Laborer William Marshall also claimed that he had overheard a bit of interplay between the killer and his victim which would have neatly fit into any number of Victorian melodramas. "I did not take much notice of them," Marshall related. "I was standing there some time and he was kissing her. I heard the man say to the deceased, 'You would say anything but your prayers.' He was mild-speaking and appeared to be an educated man. They went down the street."

The public gullibly accepted the mélange of *Police Gazette* descriptions, with composite pencil drawing, which resubstantiated their own impression of the murderer as dark-complexioned with a full face and broad shoulders. It was almost as if they wished to avoid the obvious implication that the killer might have a fair complexion and be a respectable-looking Englishman. Such a conclusion would have jolted their black and white morality, but might have forced them to deal realistically with the situation. In the meantime Sir Charles Warren appealed to their imagination by announcing that he was going to use bloodhounds to track down the killer. He was seen at 7 A.M. in Regent's Park exercising two of these dogs which *The Times* described as "magnificent animals." Across a dense coating of hoarfrost, the hounds were reported as successfully tracking a man, who had been given a fifteen-minute headstart, for over a mile. In Hyde Park that same evening, Warren held them on a leash ("as would be the case if they were employed in Whitechapel," *The Times* noted) and sent them on half a dozen hunts. Sir Melville Macnaghten would later expose Charles Warren's colorful method of allaying the public's apprehension that nothing was being done: "It should have been obvious that bloodhounds were useless in Whitechapel. I cannot conceive of a more impossible locality in which to expect hounds to work." Charles Warren was aware of that. But his cleverly perpetrated ruse would serve later to show how even the most modern techniques had been attempted, and yet had failed to catch the murderer.

One member of the press noticed that there were fewer detectives now on duty. "How do you know?" Warren retorted. "The chief value of a detective lies in the fact that you don't recognize him when you see him." Warren then published an article in *Murray's Magazine* castigating the city's newspapers by comparing them with the press on the Continent:

Across the Channel the police are masters of the situation; the public gives way before them, and the press does not venture to discuss their operations, to embarrass and hinder their inquiries or to publish their results.

His own desire for secrecy and power was growing, as he recalled the riots of 1886:

If we search history during the present century, we shall find that down to 1886 [the year prior to his being knighted after his soldiers, armed with bayonets, attacked the demonstrators in Trafalgar Square] the mob or rabble exercised a decided influence over the destinies of London.

He then assaulted the average Londoner as being fickle toward the police:

This violently fickle conduct is endangering the discipline of the force, encouraging the mob to disorder and rapine . . .

What he now encouraged was ultimately a police state:

It is deplorable that successive governments have not had the courage to make a stand against the more noisy section of these people, and it is still more to be regretted that ex-Ministers, now in Opposition,* have not hesitated to embarrass those in power by smiling on the insurgent mob.

All of this barrage was intended to distract from the more involved problem which haunted Sir Charles Warren day and night. Something had to be done quickly about a certain member of the Royal Family.

---

* Namely, William Ewart Gladstone, leader of the Liberal Party in Parliament, who was totally out of favor with the Queen.

Chapter 7

THE QUEEN AND
HER GRANDSON

Overlooking Balmoral Castle, hidden behind a screen of rare conifers and forest trees, was a small tree-capped hill with a cairn bearing the inscription:

> To the beloved memory of Albert the Great and Good, Prince Consort, erected by his brokenhearted widow, Victoria R.

While Edward, Prince of Wales, was growing into manhood, Queen Victoria had written to him, constantly restating her hope that he might be like his father:

> You may join us in thanking God for joining to us all your dearest, perfect Father . . . you can *ever* be proud enough of being the *child* of such a Father who has not his *equal* in this world—so great, so good, so faultless.

Meanwhile, in a letter to her daughter Victoria, Prussian Crown Prince Friedrich Wilhelm's wife, the Queen confided about Edward, "He is so idle and weak."

The young Prince of Wales was desperately bored. After Oxford University, his father continued to hound him to be not only a gentleman, but "the first gentleman" of the realm. Finally, it was Lord Torrington, one of the great gossips of London, who first brought to the Prince Consort "the story current in the Clubs," that a liaison existed between the Prince of Wales and an actress. It was a tremendous blow to Prince Albert's self-esteem and he wrote to his son that it "has caused me the greatest pain I have yet felt in this life."

Shortly thereafter he wrote to his daughter Princess Alice: "I am at a very low ebb. Much worry and great sorrow has robbed me of my sleep during the past fortnight. In this shattered state I had a very heavy catarrh and for the past four days am suffering from headache and pains in my limbs which may develop into rheumatism."

They were symptoms of typhoid. After collapsing on December 2, Prince Albert died at 11 P.M. on December 14, 1861. The Prince of Wales, who had been taking year-end examinations, had reached Windsor at three o'clock the morning of the next day. But his mother refused to see him. He soon learned that it was the Queen's absolute conviction that he had caused his father's death.

In total depression, the young prince returned to his studies while Queen Victoria wrote to her daughter Victoria, the Crown Princess of Prussia:

> Bertie [her nickname for the Prince of Wales]—oh, that Boy—much as I pity, I never can or shall look at him without a shudder, as you may imagine—he does not know that I know all . . . all the disgusting details . . .

The Crown Princess of Prussia pleaded with her mother to forgive the Prince of Wales, but Victoria wrote back:

> . . . if you had seen [the Prince Consort] struck down, day by day get worse and finally die, I doubt if you could bear the sight of the one who was the cause; or if you would not feel, as I do, a shudder . . . I feel daily, hourly, something which is dreadful to describe. Pity him, I do . . . But more you cannot ask. This dreadful cross kills me!

Her refusal to forgive became resolute, even though her husband's old friend Colonel Francis Seymour tried most delicately to reason with her that Prince Albert's "extraordinary pureness of mind" had caused him to take deeply to heart, more than a normal father would have done, "a youthful error that very few young men escape," and that it was impossible "to hope that the Prince of Wales should avoid."

Victoria, at this point, could not stand her son's presence near her. She decided, therefore, that he should be dispatched as quickly as possible upon a journey to Palestine and the Near East.* "Bertie's journey is all settled," the Queen wrote to the Crown Princess. "Many wished to shake my resolution and to keep him here, to force a constant contact which is more than ever unbearable to me . . ."

The Queen's wishes were carried out. In addition, she urged that upon his return he should be married. A suitable wife had been chosen, Princess Alexandra of Denmark, even though Edward had declared uncompromisingly, prior to his father's death, that he would marry only for love.

At the wedding service, the bride, all of seventeen, with brown curls and luminous pool-like brown eyes, reportedly looked very lovely in a white satin gown trimmed with garlands of orange blossom and puffings of white tulle with lace. The Prince of Wales, plump and nervous, dressed in Garter robes and gold collar over a general's uniform, according to one attendant, looked for the first time like "the first gentleman" of the realm. The radiance of the scene was enhanced by the costumes of attendant beefeaters and heralds, and by the coats of gold cloth worn by the State trumpeters who announced the arrivals of the separate processions of clergy, Knights of the Garter, royalties, and the bride.

* An extended journey or voyage was used often by the Royal Family. The Prince and Princess of Wales sent Eddy and his younger brother, George, on a series of three cruises aboard H.M.S. *Bacchante* when they no longer wished to have them near. It was on the second of these cruises, in Australia, when Eddy, age eighteen, contracted what his tutor, the Reverend Dalton, described in his diary as "a trifling ailment," but which later was diagnosed by Sir William Gull as syphilis.

93

The Prince of Wales glanced nervously at his mother, who took no part in the ceremony.

Prior to the service, which was held in St. George's Chapel, Windsor, on March 10, 1863, the Queen had conducted her son and his newly betrothed into the mausoleum at Frogmore where Prince Albert was buried. Joining their hands over her husband's casket, Victoria murmured, *"He* gives you his blessing!"

Victoria decreed that wherever her subjects should gather together, they should be reminded of "Albert the Great and Good." All over the country, at Aberdeen, at Perth, at Wolverhampton, statues of the Prince Consort were erected, which the Queen unveiled herself. But the most overwhelming "reminder" was constructed in Kensington Gardens. At first, there was some confusion in Victoria's mind as to whether it should be a statue or an institution of some kind. She finally decided on a granite obelisk with sculptures at its base.

After three years of constant toil by workmen, the memorial was still far from being completed. But finally, its one hundred and seventy life-size figures, in a frieze two hundred feet in length, were chiseled. Four enormous statues representing the greater Christian virtues and four additional colossal statues representing the greater moral values were raised in their midst. And eight bronzes symbolizing Astronomy, Chemistry, Geology, Geometry, Rhetoric, Medicine, Philosophy, and Physiology were fastened to glittering pinnacles high in the air above. In the center of the elaborate construction was placed a statue of bronze gilt, weighing nearly ten tons. "I have chosen the sitting position," commented the architect, Gilbert Scott, "as best conveying the idea of dignity befitting a royal personage." The word "Albert" on its base was felt to be sufficient to identify it.

In the years since the death of her husband, the Queen had been obsessed by his memory. She kept his bedroom exactly as it had been during his lifetime. The bed was made fresh every day, his frilled nightshirt was laid out each night on the starched pillow, and hot water for his shaving was carried up each morning.

Even the chamber pot was taken out of its bedside cupboard each night and placed beneath his bed.

Victoria's life became a lonely vigil. Dressed in black, she traveled mournfully from Windsor to Osborne, from Osborne to Balmoral. She kept to herself, where she alone could feel her departed consort's mysterious presence.

As the Queen's madness grew, she began seeing a medium, Robert James Lees. How Lees came into her life and eventually affected the ominous career of her grandson was curious.

Lees, a young man in his teens, had been reported as receiving messages from Prince Albert. The existence of the medium was brought to Victoria's attention by James Burns, the editor of a popular psychic newspaper. She dispatched two members of her court, secretly and anonymously, to call on Lees.

When the two emissaries from the Queen entered the medium's room, he greeted them normally. Suddenly the dead Prince Consort's voice was apparently heard coming from Lee's lips, saying, "You are Lord _____ and you are the Earl of _____" identities which they had not yet acknowledged. Then the Prince, still controlling Lees, shook their hands, giving a secret and advanced Masonic grip which the young medium would have no way of knowing. A personal message was conveyed which was to be transmitted to the Queen with facts and details only Victoria would be able to confirm. Finally, as an irresistible proof of identity, he wrote a note and signed it with a name he used only when corresponding privately with his wife.

Robert James Lees was summoned to the Palace where he arranged a séance. This was held in 1863, the year of Eddy's birth. During the séance, the Queen maintained she was able, finally, to communicate with the spirit of her dear dead Albert. She invited Lees to enter her service, so that he might be available to her at all times. But Lees declined the offer. Instead he gave the Queen a communication from Albert that there was a man already in her service who could act as a medium and maintain the link that had been provided. That man was John Brown.

Finally in touch with her dead husband, Victoria decided that she must follow his wishes in all things. She sat from morning till dark at her desk reading and writing letters. With utter dedication, she would work as *he* had worked, in the service of their country.

John Brown slept in her neighboring bedchamber at night. Through him, Prince Albert's presence was available to her at all times. When the Prince Consort's spirit, through Brown, abruptly commanded her to get off her pony or put on her shawl, she meekly obeyed. Those around her were stunned, but Victoria became completely dependent on her servant. He was a legacy from the dead and two gold medals were struck in his honor. Even Prime Minister Disraeli was careful to send personal messages to "Mr. Brown" in his letters to the Queen.

Shortly after her marriage to Albert, Victoria had been fired at in the street with a pistol by a young man named Edward Oxford. Although she was not injured, Oxford was convicted of high treason, declared insane, and committed to an asylum for life.

The Prince Consort was unhappy with the verdict. Two years later, when John Francis also tried to shoot the Queen, and pleaded insane, Prince Albert proclaimed that there was no insanity involved. "The wretched creature," he remarked, "is not out of his mind but a thorough scamp. I hope his trial will be conducted with the greatest strictness."

The jurors concurred with Albert and the plea of insanity was set aside. Francis was found guilty of high treason and condemned to death.

In 1882, while she was walking from a train to her royal carriage, a nineteen-year-old youth named Roderick Maclean fired a pistol at Victoria from a few yards. An Eton boy struck Maclean's arm with an umbrella before the pistol discharged. The Queen was unharmed.

Maclean was arrested immediately and subsequently tried for high treason. The jury brought in a verdict of "not guilty, but insane" and Maclean was sent to an asylum.

Victoria, remembering Albert's disapproval of a similar verdict in the case of Edward Oxford, challenged the jury. What did they mean, she demanded, by saying that Maclean was not guilty—she had seen him fire the pistol himself. In vain her constitutional advisors reminded her of the principle of English Law which stated that no man could be found guilty of a crime unless he was shown to have had a criminal intention. Victoria was unconvinced. "If that is the law," she replied, "the law must be altered." And altered it was. In 1883, an Act was passed changing the form of the verdict in cases of insanity to either "guilty" or "innocent." It was a confusing juxtaposition, one that seemed to defy not only British Law, but all the laws of logic. Yet it remained on the Statute Book and no one from that day onward challenged its coherence.

One wonders how far Victoria would have had to bend the bonds of logic to interpret her grandson's acts if she had known he was the Whitechapel murderer. With her memory of Prince Albert's attitude and her constant contact with the faint tremblings which he still emitted, how deeply might she have been torn by Eddy's actions! If he were actually declared guilty before a British court and had been faced with a sentence of death, would she not have been moved by something inside her to plead on behalf of his insanity, hoping that it might bring about his committal to an asylum? Obviously she would have been loath to trace the origins of Eddy's mental condition. Most probably it would have seemed out of the question to her that it should have been directly affected by her own presence.

To Eddy, Victoria had always been a terrifying figure. He had seen his own father cower before her. Once at Osborne, the Prince of Wales was late for a dinner party and Eddy had discovered him standing behind a pillar, wiping the sweat from his forehead, trying to build up enough nerve to present himself to the Queen. When at last he had approached her, she gave him a cold nod, whereupon he immediately vanished behind another pillar remaining there until the party broke up.

Eddy, himself, hated her. She constantly questioned him and made disquieting remarks about his appearance, at the same time, wanting to know why he did this or that, or didn't do something, or why he thought as he did about such and such. Her presence, dressed in constant black, filled him with intense depression. Yet he treated her always with a smile and a gracious tone in his voice that seemed to trick her into believing that he admired and cared for her, while it required all his efforts to disguise his true feeling: the intoxicating rage he experienced in her presence.

On an afternoon shortly after the double murders of Elizabeth Stride and Catherine Eddowes, the Queen and her grandson had lunch at the Palace. Earlier that morning a petition had been smuggled onto her breakfast tray through the efforts of Liberal politician Leonard Courtney. Signed by four thousand women living in Whitechapel, it was addressed to "Our Most Gracious Sovereign Lady." A pathetic document, largely the work of Henrietta Barnett, wife of the Reverend Samuel A. Barnett of Toynbee Hall, it was the plea of many women to the one woman in England who might be able to accomplish something:

> Madam, we, the women of East London, feel horror at the dreadful sins that have been lately committed in our midst, and grief because of the shame that has befallen our neighbourhood. By the facts which have come out in the inquests, we have learnt much of the lives of our sisters who have lost a firm hold on goodness and who are living sad and degraded lives.

> While each woman of us will do all she can to make men feel with horror the sins of impurity which cause such wicked lives to be led, we also beg that your Majesty will call on your servants in authority and bid them put the law which already exists in motion to close bad houses within whose walls such wickedness is done and men and women ruined in body and soul.

> We are, Madam, your loyal and humble servants.

Victoria had become a collector. She had given orders to her servants that nothing should ever be thrown away. In drawer after drawer, in wardrobe after wardrobe, reposed her dresses of seventy years. On the walls at Windsor were portraits of all her relatives, revealing them at every age. No carpet, no curtain could be replaced by another unless its pattern was so identically reproduced that the keenest eyes might not detect the difference. All her belongings—the furs and mantles, the muffs, the parasols and bonnets—were accounted for in chronological order and dated. Every article in her possession was photographed from several points of view. These photographs were placed in a series of richly bound volumes, an entry was made indicating the number of the article, the number of the room in which it was kept, its exact position in the room, and its principal characteristics. She collected her children and grandchildren, as well. She wanted to know each detail of their lives and her decision was final as to how they should conduct themselves.

When Eddy arrived for lunch, the Queen, after a few moments, realized that he was not well. She had asked about his father, who was still on the Continent, and about his younger brother, George, but then noticed that Eddy was not responding at all. When she inquired as to his pale face and trembling hands, he complained that he had a severe headache.

She had long been concerned about Eddy's health. In the past few months, he had seemed to be dissipating terribly. She believed that it was time he should be married and had written of this to her son, the Prince of Wales. Indeed, there were plans moving in that direction.

The most favorable would be Princess Margaret, nicknamed "Mossy," her granddaughter and Eddy's cousin, the youngest sister of Kaiser Wilhelm II. The problem then, however, was "Bertie's" worsening relationship with the House of Hanover. Another possibility was her granddaughter Princess Alix of Hesse, another cousin of Eddy's. She would suggest both names to her son in the hope that something could be done to aid poor Eddy in his obvious distress.

Once married, the color would return to poor little Eddy's cheeks and his thin hands would stop shaking. But in the meantime she suggested to him that he be examined by Dr. Gull.

In 1869, "Bertie" had been mixed up in that ugly Mordaunt scandal which had been created when Lady Mordaunt informed her husband that she had been unfaithful with the Prince of Wales. Unfortunately "Bertie" had written letters to Lady Mordaunt and they were produced at the divorce trial.

The Prince of Wales had immediately become the object of several attacks and one of them, entitled *The Coming of K,* which parodied Tennyson's popular *Idylls of the King*, pictured him as unfit to succeed to the throne.

Victoria had pleaded with "Bertie" not to appear at the trial, but he had defied her in writing: "Dear Alix has entirely taken the same view in the matter that I have and quite sees that it is an absolute necessity for me to appear in court, should I be called."

He *was* called, and was asked by the court:

> *Has there ever been any improper familiarity or criminal act between yourself and Lady Mordaunt?*

The Prince of Wales's response was firm:

> *I have not.*

But at the opera that evening the audience rose and applauded Princess Alexandra in the Royal Box and then hissed when the Prince appeared.

In November 1871, possibly because of the tension from the never-ending divorce proceedings and the public pressure mounting against him, "Bertie" had contracted typhoid at Lord Landesborough's house near Scarborough. Dr. Gull, then an unknown physician, was called in to pull him through.

The Times of December 18 described how:

> In Dr. Gull were combined energy that never tired, watchfulness that never flagged; nursing so tender, ministry so minute, that in his functions he seemed to combine the duties of physician, dresser, dispenser, valet, nurse,—now arguing with the sick man in his delirium so softly and pleasantly that the parched lips opened to take the scanty nourishment on which depended the reserves of strength for the deadly fight when all else failed, now lifting the wasted body from bed to bed, now washing the worn frame with vinegar, with ever ready eye and ear and finger to mark any change and phase, to watch face and heart and pulse, and passing at times twelve or fourteen hours at that bedside.

In 1872, Victoria, in appreciation for Gull's saving the Prince of Wales from death, named him Sir William Gull, Bart. Later in the same year she appointed Gull Physician Extraordinary to the

Queen. From that day forward, Dr. Gull had been regarded as chief physician to the Royal Family, although he specialized mainly in nervous disorders. But Victoria continually relied on his medical skills, so without hesitation, on that afternoon following the murders of Elizabeth Stride and Catherine Eddowes, she summoned Gull to the Palace to treat her grandson.

But Gull was not able to come. The stroke that he had suffered the year before had left him partially paralyzed so that now he was hardly able to leave his home at 74 Brook Street, Grosvenor Square West. Eddy would have to go to him. Victoria, as she did with all of her court, her children, and her grandchildren, immediately ordered that he go there, and Eddy, without comment, was impelled to obey.

Chapter 8

GULL

William Withey Gull was born at Colchester in the parish of St. Leonard's on December 31, 1816. His father died of cholera when William was ten, leaving him to be raised by his strict, churchgoing mother, Elizabeth. On Fridays they ate fish and rice pudding; in Lent, she wore black, and all saint's holidays were rigidly observed.

William was sent to a school kept by a clergyman, and when he came home each afternoon he was never allowed to play until he did a certain number of rows of knitting. Thus, William knitted the first pair of socks he ever wore.

As he grew into young manhood, most probably to escape the bleak household and his mother's strong religious views, William desperately longed to go to sea. Elizabeth Gull confided to her friend, a Mr. Harrison, who was a nephew of the treasurer of Guy's Hospital, that she was troubled by her son's desire to leave home. Harrison met with William and encouraged him to become a doctor. He began training the boy in classical studies. However, on his free days, William would row down the estuary to the sea and watch the fishermen obtaining the mysterious living treasures that teemed in the nets of the dredgers along the coast. Often he would collect specimens, which he carefully studied with the aid of such books as he could procure. Afterward he would look upon this time as the happiest period of his youth.

At twenty-one, William Gull, through Mr. Harrison's influence, began residence at Guy's Hospital. From then on, his life was lived within the wards of the hospital. At all hours of the day and night, he could be found by some bedside seeking patiently to unravel the mysteries of disease. In 1846 he took the M.D. degree at the University of London, gaining a gold medal, the highest honor which the University conferred.

Yet, despite his great ability, he had a remarkable lack of confidence in his own powers. During the final examination he panicked and was about to leave the room, saying that he knew nothing of the case proposed for comment. Fortunately, a friend persuaded him to return, with the result that the thesis he wrote earned for him both his Doctor's degree and the gold medal.

"I do not know," he often remarked when faced with a new patient or a set of symptoms which he could not readily identify. Above all, he considered himself a clinical physician. He often recalled his favorite saying: "Fools and savages explain; wise men investigate."

He wrote in his journal:

> If the first lesson be patience, . . . the next lesson is docility, a readiness to learn at any source, . . . wherever the facts lie hid . . . who could have believed that the particles of a dew-drop and the masses of a planet are moulded and controlled by the same force; that the introduction into the human body of a small particle of matter from a cow's udder might be the means of saving thousands of human lives? We learn from these and innumerable similar instances that the highest truths lie hid in the simplest facts; that, unlike human proclamations, nature's teachings are not by sound of trumpet, but often in the stillest voice . . .

The difficulty, however, is in maintaining the docile spirit of which I speak, in preventing ourselves from assuming a knowledge we have not; in not hastily coming to a conclusion without evidence, and not resting content in our ignorance with a fool's satisfaction that no good would come of more knowledge if we had it.

But it was his manner which distinguished Dr. Gull. Especially when it came to handling the rich and titled. A passage from Guy's Hospital Reports described:

His striking presence, his searching scrutiny, his minute and deliberate examination of every case, and the few carefully and slowly uttered words in which he delivered his judgement, sometimes with epigrammatic pungency, often with encouragement, and never without sympathy—all combined to give him an almost unequalled ascendancy over his patients. It was just the same in a hospital ward as in a palace . . . the richest were taught to restrain loquacity, to answer truthfully, and to follow out directions implicitly.

William Gull's introduction into the Royal Family came through his friend, Henry Acland. In September 1859, when Prince Albert refused to let the Prince of Wales live as an ordinary undergraduate at Oxford, but demanded that he reside in a private residence with his governor, Major-General Bruce, and an equerry, Major Teesdale, *Punch* was moved to print some verses entitled "A Prince at High Pressure," which began:

Thou dear little Wales, sure the saddest of tales
Is the tale of the studies with which they are cramming
 thee

However, the Prince of Wales was spared having to live with a private physician as well, when Henry Acland, then Oxford's Regius Professor of Medicine, agreed to accept responsibility for his health. Acland continued to look after the Prince, and in 1860 accompanied him on a tour to the United States. Their arrival in New York City was described by Major-General Bruce:

The reception at New York has thrown all its predecessors into the shade. I despair of its being understood in England . . . Believe me, however, that exaggeration is impossible . . . the affair has been one of continual triumph.

The Prince of Wales, accompanied by Acland and New York Mayor Fernando Wood, was driven down Broadway in a barouche, specially built for the occasion, while thousands cheered. As he stood high above the crowd and bowed from the balcony of his suite at the Fifth Avenue Hotel, the Prince of Wales remarked to Mayor Wood that his rooms were far more comfortable than the ones in which he lived at Buckingham Palace and Windsor Castle.

In 1868, Henry Acland had met William Gull at Oxford. Gull gave an address at the meeting of the British Medical Association entitled "Clinical Observation in Relation to Medicine in Modern Times" in which he stated the one theme which underscored his work:

Medicine is a specialism, but of no narrow kind. We have to dissect nature, which for practice is better than to abstract it. Every form of life has to us a value, but in an order the reverse of the generalisations of natural history. We desire to know what limits, specialises, and perverts. We study in order to distinguish, and not to classify.

Afterward, Acland and Gull became close friends. In 1871, when the Prince of Wales contracted typhoid and lay near death, Acland, who still felt responsible for the Prince's health, did not hesitate to call in Gull and entrust him with the Prince's condition.

Sir William Gull, in return, owed much to Henry Acland. And, as will be seen, his involvement with the Acland family carried over into the tragic series of events which were about to overwhelm both his private life and his professional career. He was about to become a conspirator in order to preserve his Queen and perpetuate the existing British Government.*

* It was ironic that Sir William Gull should have also treated Eddy's lover, James Stephen. On the afternoon following his accident, when he was

After Prince Albert Victor, affectionately known to his family and close friends as "Eddy," arrived at the house at 74 Brook Street, Sir William Gull led him into the private parlor which he used for receiving patients. Gull could still get around, but the stroke he had suffered the year before made it impossible to treat patients outside his home.

He carefully examined the young man. The Prince's long thin face and penetrating eyes stared back at him, and his hands shook when he did not keep them clasped together. His appearance revealed symptoms of extreme dementia as his left hand with its thick gold band on the last finger tightly clenched the fingers of his right. From the young man's complaint of headaches and the evidence of chronic suppuration about the ear, Gull immediately recognized that he was suffering from syphilitic cachexia.†

---

knocked off his horse by the windmill blade, James first had been taken to a local physician and then to his father's house at 32 De Vere Gardens, where Gull examined him. Although it was reported that James made a full recovery, Gull treated him for the flashes of pain and inability to concentrate which he continued to experience.

Gull had become the most prominent physician in England, while within a few decades, through pure force of will, the Stephen family had also taken their place as respected members of Britain's ruling class.

James's great-grandfather had begun as an evidence collector for a firm of solicitors, and after gathering evidence against Queen Caroline and for Sir Fowell Buxton's inquiry into the slave trade, had managed to rise to the position of Master in Chancery, becoming finally a Member of Parliament. His son Sir James Stephen began as Colonial Secretary in 1822, and, after contributing to *The Edinburgh Review*, was appointed Professor of Modern History at Cambridge. His son was Sir James Fitzjames Stephen, Bart., K.C.S.I., a distinguished lawyer and codifier of the Indian legal system. He, too, contributed to such socially conscious journals as *The Saturday Review* and *The Pall-Mall Gazette*. At the end of the line was James K. Stephen, who was henceforth to be known as the one who gave the English language one of its most famous soubriquets. In Scotland children were already skipping rope in singsong to:

> Jack the Ripper's dead,
> And lying on his bed.
> He cut his throat
> With sunlight soap . . .
> Jack the Ripper's dead.

† Dr. Gull's treatment of a prior case of syphilis was commented on in a treatise by Sir Jonathan Hutchinson, the foremost authority on syphilis in England during the late 1800s: "If we may count Sir William Gull's case as the first in which pathological appearances were noticed, we have in it the record

Syphilitic cachexia was a condition he, himself, had compared in a recent address at Oxford to epilepsy as a form of cerebral disease. But it was not the sort of information that could readily be passed on to Her Royal Majesty. Not just yet.

The element that troubled Dr. Gull was Eddy's eyes, their stare. He wanted to look behind them. They suggested something beyond the physical symptoms which he had observed—an unexplored area. As an expert in nervous disorders, he had long felt that merely treating the physical symptoms of disease often left certain other implications open to question. He had cited this gap in

---

of inflammatory changes in the cord which were appreciable only to the microscope."

Syphilis had already been identified as a generalized systemic disease initiated by a microorganism known as *Spirochaeta pallida* or *Treponema pallidum*, and although the organism could be killed by various chemicals, once entering the body tissues, it was believed to remain alive for the lifetime of the infected person. Since its first appearance in the early seventeenth century, its signs and symptoms (lesions of the skin and mouth) had been recognized, its infectiousness was proven, and the means of transmission were well known.

Although mercury was widely used in treating syphilis, iodide of potassium, which was first introduced in 1834, was found to be often more effective in treating younger men.

It was already a proven fact that there was definitely more syphilis and more hazard of infection in low social-economic groups; however, transmission could take place when habits, customs, and attitudes of people caused them to have sexual relations with infected persons.

After the spirochete gained admission to the body, usually through sexual intercourse, it reproduced itself at the admission site and within hours began to spread through the blood stream, although symptoms did not generally appear until after about twenty-one days. The highly infectious sore that resulted was either extremely pronounced or so slight as to go unnoticed. Even without treatment, this sore could heal without a scar, but the disease was still rampant in the body.

As the condition advanced, it was accompanied by gradual changes in personality. These often included delusions, loss of memory, apathy, and disorientation. Sir William Gull, as Sir Jonathan Hutchinson had remarked, was the first physician to discover the effects of syphilis on the spinal cord, or specifically, how it brought about a degeneration of the posterior columns, which subsequently was named *tabes dorsalis* or locomotor ataxia. It had already been shown that this neurosyphilitic state produced drooping of the eyelids, loss of sexual power, loss of weight, deafness, severe sudden attacks of intense abdominal pain, vomiting, and disintegration of one or more joints.

practice in his address as President of the Clinical Society in 1872:

> As medical men we know of tendencies to latent insanity without the least overt evidence of their existence; minds which on a strain will certainly give way. We know this as well as we know of weak and imperfect hearts or other viscera. The onset of acute disorders of mind or body, to use a common expression, by no means coincides with the date of their causes. This is so well established in medicine that we go back upon a latent cause from the occurrence of acute effects, feeling assured we shall find it, however previously hidden. It is only the ignorant who can overlook these connections.

In his desire to uncover the "latent cause" behind Eddy's obvious physical dementia, Dr. Gull was led to make an unorthodox decision. He would hypnotize the young man who sat before him.

The use of hypnotism in medical practice had been severely attacked since its inception in the early part of the century. George Corfe, apothecary of Middlesex Hospital, had labeled it "the work of the devil." *The Lancet*, in a recent article, had strongly concurred:

> We regard its abettors as quacks and impostors; they ought to be hooted out of professional society.

But Dr. Gull was neither a quack nor an impostor. He had found hypnotism especially useful in treating dipsomania, as on almost every occasion it developed within the patient a complete aversion to alcohol.

But in cases of nervous disorders it was even more effective when used to explore those areas which were often the cause of physical symptoms whose motivations seemed indefinable.

Dr. Gull rarely used drugs. In fact, he found their addiction often more harmful than the disease itself. His approach was nearly always investigative, as he once remarked, "treating the disease, never the diseased patient."

His use of hypnosis was the most modern and simplified: known as the Nancy Method. He sat Eddy in an easy chair with his back to the light. Standing behind him, Gull held the index and middle fingers of his right hand about six inches in front of Eddy's face and a little above his eyes. With a murmur, he told Eddy to look at his fingers and not think of anything. Beginning in a low monotonous voice, Gull intoned:

You are beginning . . . to feel sleepy . . . to want to sleep . . . your sight is getting dim . . . my fingers are getting indistinct . . . your eyelids are drooping . . . your eyes are closing . . . sleep . . . sleep . . .

Once again, Gull repeated the instructions in the same low voice. In a moment or two, Eddy's eyes began to blink. They closed for a second, and then reopened sluggishly, closed again, and finally reopened—until Gull reached over and gently closed them, holding the lids shut with his fingers—as he continued to repeat:

You want to sleep . . . it's growing dark . . . sleep . . . sleep . . .

For a long time Gull sat with his patient, even though the young man had already entered into a deep trance. Just as Gull had patiently investigated the diseases of so many others in an attempt to uncover the cause, rather than merely to treat the physical symptoms, he methodically began his questions.

Eddy told him first about James, then about the anger he felt toward his father. Finally his eyes became like glass as he recalled another image, one that filled Gull with alarm. It was "the knife" he referred to and the woman in the darkness.

Gull watched in horror as Eddy showed him how he slit the woman's throat. The phantom knife descended with a sudden thrust down.

"Why?" Gull asked.

But Eddy could only repeat what he had told him. He repeated it as if something inside him were stuck on that image. Finally Gull made him stop. There was no point in going on.

Sir William Gull had discovered the "latent cause" for Eddy's demented state. The syphilis had thrust him into fits of fantastic rage. Violence was the outpouring of his pain.

But in Eddy's case, it was not simply fantasy. He had reenacted the obsessions that he felt. The madness which had overtaken his being was a perpetual state of delirium. He was not mentally responsible, yet the acts had been committed.

Gull had no alternative but to let this information be known. Which is why he communicated to Sir Charles Warren that he had to see him immediately.

Charles Warren was pictured as a dupe. A cartoon in *Punch* caricatured him wearing his military hat, riding a hobby horse into battle while a small ragged boy standing by the entrance to an alley called out: "Mr. Policeman, there's a murder round the corner!" Another cartoon showed Warren, Home Secretary Henry Matthews, and Lord Salisbury engaged in a bitter argument, captioned:

> MATTHEWS (to Warren): "Why don't you resign!"
> WARREN (to Matthews): "Why don't *you* resign!"
> SALISBURY (aside): "Why don't they *both* resign!"

On Guy Fawkes Night there was a clash between rioters and police on Clerkenwell Green. The police confiscated a scarecrow. It turned out to be an effigy of Sir Charles Warren which a group of Socialists planned to burn.

There was never a more blurred picture of a government official than the one the public now accepted of their Metropolitan Police Commissioner. Sir Charles was referred to as if he were the butt of a joke, a man "on a hobby horse," outsmarted at every turn by the cunningly insidious demoniacal monster-fiend who prowled Whitechapel cutting down whores.

Londoners mercilessly recalled the image of Warren in his stovepipe hat marching on the "Bloody Sunday" strikers:

> *Mounted upon his gallant steed,*
> *The Chief Commissionaire*
> *Of Britain's Bobbies took the lead*
> *In crammed Trafalgar Square.*
> *Despite the threatened signs of war,*
> *He came to guard the "show,"*
> *And socialistic hearts o'erawe*
> *By wearing his chapeau.*

All honour to his Mightiness,
Who readily foresaw
How forcibly civilian dress
Would emphasize the law!
Never can perish Warren's name,
Though ages come and go;
And handed down to deathless fame
Will be that dread chapeau!

Four days following the murders of Elizabeth Stride and Catherine Eddowes, Sir Charles, in a long, detailed letter published in *The Times*, retaliated to the charge that he had switched experienced detectives from one district to another where they did not know the locale, and thus were unable to police the area. Also, he insisted that he had not changed the old system of beat patrols but was at present utilizing the same system that had been in existence for the past twenty years.

Warren, in reality, was neither a fool nor incompetent in his duties. He was an extremely clever man who was always several steps ahead of his adversaries. But at this point, he found himself involved in a grander scheme than trying to hold on to his job as Police Commissioner.

He had agreed to meet Sir William Gull at Gull's Grosvenor Square residence. When Warren arrived, Gull conducted him into the same private parlor in which Eddy had been hypnotized. Gull then proceeded to tell Warren of his discovery. He related how he had put the Prince in a trance and while in this state the young man had reenacted the Whitechapel killings. There was no question in Gull's mind that the details were authentic. In addition, the Prince had implicated his former tutor, James K. Stephen, as the author of the letters to the Central News Agency which bore the signature "Jack the Ripper."

Warren listened intently and then confronted Gull with an astonishing revelation. Not only was he aware of Prince Eddy's murderous activities; this knowledge had been shared with Home Secretary Matthews and with the Prime Minister as well!

It was imperative that the Queen should not be informed, but that her grandson be isolated until the Prince of Wales could be told and appropriate protective measures be taken.

But how was this to be accomplished? Since arrest was out of the question, Sir Charles Warren asked Dr. Gull if he had a suggestion.

Dr. Gull's diagnosis of the Prince's syphilitic condition prompted immediate medical care. This could be accomplished in relative secrecy, if, in fact, the patient were confined to a private sanitarium. Gull's best source was Sir Henry Acland's son, Dr. Theodore Dyke Acland, Physician to St. Thomas's Hospital and to the House of Rest Sanitarium in Balham. Theodore Acland resided nearby at 7 Brook Street and was engaged to Gull's daughter, Caroline.

Warren agreed to the idea. Balham was a quiet village, hardly more than a railway stop. There the Prince could be treated in secret.

Chapter 9

THE CONSPIRATORS

Lord Salisbury did not believe in a legislative government, but in a class born to rule. Self-control he regarded as the noblest and most important of the civic virtues. Legislation, in short, could not improve the individual.

However, when conditions in the East End were deplored as unlivable, he took his place on the Royal Commission with the Prince of Wales and warmly advocated state expenditure in dealing with the evils of overcrowding. Some of his aristocratic friends accused him of turning Socialist, but Salisbury replied in a typically contradictory manner:

> My noble friend may press as earnestly as he will upon the necessity of leaving every Englishman to work out his own destiny, and not attempt to aid him at the expense of the State; but, on the other side, he must bear in mind that there are no absolute truths or principles in politics.

Perhaps *there were* "no absolute truths or principles" but Salisbury was firmly against organic change and worked for the continued existence of an aristocratic ruling class.

His devotion to Her Royal Majesty was chivalrous. Being the first of her Prime Ministers who was younger than she, Salisbury listened with almost child-like awe to her views on foreign and domestic policy. Victoria, in return, found him to be animated by the same notions as she herself—an acute sense of obligation, strong devotion to duty, and a constant regard for English traditions. Eventually she coaxed him with the offer of a dukedom, which he respectfully declined.

In the general election of 1880, when Disraeli was heavily defeated, Lord Salisbury had succeeded him as leader in the House of Lords, sharing leadership of the Conservative Party as a whole with Sir Stafford Northcote. He continued the war against Gladstone and his Liberals by branding them "theorists" and "phrasemakers" when it came to economic stability. Speaking continually from public platforms across the country, Salisbury emphasized that "unity" and "mutual trust" were the indispensable foundations for all moral and material welfare in a nation.

"How long can the final disintegration of the Empire be postponed?" he wrote in an article published by the *Quarterly*. A dangerous breach was forming, caused by the new class-conscious Radicals, "those who lead the poorer classes, industriously impressing upon them that the function of legislation is to transfer to them something from the pockets of their more fortunate fellow-countrymen." He championed the "sacredness of property" and expressed a strong preference for the old form of parliamentary government which was controlled by the Crown and the aristocracy. The "people," he remarked, are "a myth."

Early in 1888, Salisbury had introduced a measure in the House of Lords for the creation of fifty life peers, to be drawn from the ranks of the judges, governors, ambassadors, and high-ranking officers of the Army, Navy, and Civil Service. He felt that the House of Lords was the one body freed from the evil of its members being subject to re-election. Thus, it existed to provide a check on any hasty legislation which might otherwise be passed on through the House of Commons.

England's ruling class must be preserved at any cost, Salisbury insisted; however, he was critical of the nobly born who failed to respond to the obligations of their station. They must exert themselves or atrophy.

His strongest conviction was that the principal function of the State was to establish and maintain *absolute, unbiased* justice. But, like many men in high politics, justice was held sacred only as long as it served one's political ends. The moment it was found expeditious, laws were broken, the truth was twisted, and every attempt made to conceal the taint of guilt. It is curious that at the time of the Ripper murders, one of the principal measures which Salisbury urged through to passage was a "policeman" Act. Viewed as a protection of the man in the street, it called for regular inspection of weighing machines.

More than anyone else in England, Charles Steward Parnell threatened the political existence of Lord Salisbury's Conservative Party. Since Parnell's election as chairman of the Irish Parliamentary Party in May 1880, both Liberals and Conservatives had alternately attempted to negotiate with him to settle the Irish question. But in 1886, Gladstone's Liberal Party came out strongly for Irish Home Rule.

This was more than Salisbury could tolerate. In a speech given at St. James's Hall, Salisbury began with an attack on Irish self-government which broadened into a diatribe against the Oriental nations, India, the Russians, and the Greeks, all of whom were doubtful repositories for the privilege of self-government. "When you come down to it," he concluded, "you will find that self-government works admirably well when it is confided to people of Teutonic race, but that it does not work so well when people of other races are called upon to join in it." The address was interrupted throughout by the enthusiastic applause of his Conservative audience; and, at the close of his remarks, Salisbury went so far as to sanction the use of force by Orangemen to defend themselves.

After the general election of 1886, when Gladstone was defeated and the Conservatives were returned to power with a large majority over Liberals and Parnellites combined, Salisbury set out to crush Parnell once and for all.

Circumventing his precept of *absolute, unbiased justice,* Salisbury made an agreement with *The Times* that a series of articles would be run entitled "Parnellism and Crime" to which the Government would supply certain details. The pact was made in the utmost secrecy with George Earle Buckle, the new twenty-nine-year-old editor of *The Times,* who was as hostile to Irish Home Rule as was Salisbury, and just as determined to use any means to save the British Empire from the disaster which the Conservatives believed it faced.

The attack which *The Times* mounted against Parnell charged him with outrage and murder, implying that the Irish people were utterly unfit for self-government. Parnell was characterized as heading an organization (The Irish Parliamentary Party) "whose ultimate aim is plunder and whose ultimate sanction is murder, to paralyze the House of Commons and to hand Ireland over to social and financial ruin."

Parnell, in the manner of a cool, clear-eyed politician, did not respond. However, when a second series of *unsigned* articles were printed, entitled "Behind the Scenes in America," a Parnell associate, F. H. O'Donnell, sued *The Times* for libel.

During the libel trial, which began in July 1888, a number of incriminating letters were introduced alleged to have been written by Parnell. Parnell, speaking before the House of Commons, instantly demanded that a select committee be formed to inquire into the authenticity of these letters.

Pressure was building against the Conservative government. The tone of the hearings which took place each day indicated that Parnell had indeed been wronged by *The Time*'s reckless charges.* What the public did not know was that the *author* of those unsigned articles entitled "Behind the Scenes in America" was now solely responsible for the apprehension of Jack the Ripper.

* Since the Conservatives had co-conspired with *The Times* to destroy Parnell, *Times* editor Buckle wrote to Lord Salisbury asking whether his government might not contribute to the enormous bill of costs which the paper faced: £60,000 for witnesses alone, and a total outlay of £200,000. Salisbury, with a cunning attempt at innocence, replied that it would be "impossible and impolitic" to ask the House of Commons for money for the purpose.

When it was discovered that Sir Robert Anderson, head of the C.I.D., had not only conspired to destroy Parnell but was also in charge of catching the Ripper, who was in fact Prince Albert Victor, the explosion would not only overturn Salisbury's government, but would easily rout Britain's ruling class—her Kings, her Queens, her Princes and Lords.

The newest patient confined to the Balham House of Rest was treated in the manner which had been carefully prescribed by Sir William Gull: plenty of nourishment, which included portions of fresh fish, red meat, raw vegetables and fruits, and the administration of iodide of potassium, rather than mercury, in a wineglass of water three times a day.

Prince Albert Victor's sudden confinement was known only to Dr. Gull, Dr. Theodore Acland, Commissioner Warren, Home Secretary Matthews, and Lord Salisbury, although the Prince of Wales would soon be informed by both Gull and his own physician, Sir Henry Acland, that his son was suffering from syphilis.

To say that there was hope for recovery would have been beyond Dr. Gull's expertise to predict. At this point, his sole intent was to prevent further damage and a spread of the pathological process. From his experience it was shown that the earlier the treatment could be started after the disease's initial infection, the more effective it was in accomplishing these purposes; however, in Eddy's case, the condition had existed for almost seven years.

The fact that disturbed Gull more than any other was that he was living with a murderer, wanted by the police, and the subject of an enormous amount of publicity. Eventually, as the Ripper scare diminished from the public's consciousness, the killings might perhaps be attributed to someone else, some deranged murderer already incarcerated in an asylum or a suicide found floating in the Thames.

Commissioner Warren suggested that Dr. Gull continue to experiment in curing his royal patient through the use of electrical therapy and drugs. It was his opinion, and that of Lord Salisbury, that as long as Eddy could be safely confined, he was not a threat to the Government or the Crown.

But how long could such confinement continue before rumors began to circulate that the son of the Prince of Wales was being treated in a sanitarium for a condition more serious than "a nervous disorder?" Even the admission that he was suffering from syphilis would propagate a tremendous public uproar. It was only realistic to assume that the Prince must eventually be rehabilitated and sent about his royal duties, giving speeches and dedicating cornerstones. And what faced Gull was the overwhelming task of guarding this young man's terrible secret.

As Gull religiously studied his patient's condition, he noted that since his arrival at Balham House of Rest, the Prince did not seem to be awake most of the time. In addition, he was gradually becoming incoherent in his speech, which Gull attributed to aphasia accompanying his condition. This partial loss of power of articulate speech was not due to a defect in the peripheral organs, but to a disorder in one or more of the cerebral centers.

Within the second week of Eddy's confinement, reports began reaching Gull of a marked change in his disposition. According to the attendants assigned to his case, the Prince, with increasing regularity, was becoming wildly delirious and extremely violent in his actions.

This state was often common in syphilitic patients, but once again the "latent cause" theory presented itself to Gull. The syphilitic condition could be controlled, but not the inner torment, the madness which had driven this young man to acts of premeditated butchery. This fact would always lie heavily upon the conscience of his protectors, who were now so desperately trying to protect themselves.

Gull, at seventy-two, was a sick man. His medical career had been radiant with accomplishment, and now he was faced with having to conspire in an act so ignoble and repugnant that it haunted him. To hold an heir to the British throne captive in order to conceal the monstrous deeds for which he was responsible was taking a terrible toll. And the worst was yet to come.

The office of Lord Mayor of London dated back to the thirteenth century and the new Lord Mayor-elect, the Right Honorable James Whitehead, was about to become the recipient of all the symbolic splendor which that office held. For, in that particular square mile known as the City, he would soon take precedence over every subject of the Crown, including members of the Royal Family.

On November 9, dressed in sable-trimmed robes, the new Lord Mayor would be sworn in by the Lord Chief Justice at the Royal Law Courts in the Strand, amid all of that elegant pageantry known as the Lord Mayor's Show. Yet Lord Mayor-elect Whitehead was a refreshing change from previous holders of that office. He had decided to cut down on the pomp and circumstance involved, in order to devote the moneys saved to charity.

His action was applauded by *The Times*:

> Whitehead is opposed to the introduction of the circus element and allegorical displays, which neither accord with his tastes nor, in his opinion, with the dignity of the city.

And *Punch* added that there were to be:

> No gals in tights seated on globes . . .

Only *Reynolds News* suggested a need for a display of allegorical characters:

> Sir Charles Warren followed by a bevy of detectives blindfolded, an effigy of Jack the Ripper, and a *tableux mort* composed of the Victims of Whitechapel.

Six weeks had passed without a hint of the Ripper and Londoners were curious if, in fact, he had committed his last crime. And then, on November 7, a news article appeared in the Paris edition of the New York *Herald* which suddenly rang home:

> A woman found stabbed on the Boulevard de la Chapelle last night stated that a man attacked her and stabbed her with a knife, saying he was "Jack the Ripper" and had already killed ten women in London and two in Paris. He is believed to be mad and is still at large.

On the morning of November 8, Dr. William Gull received startling news from the Director of the Balham House of Rest. It suddenly plunged him into an intense state of fear and expectancy. During the early morning hours, the young man, who was solely under his care, had suffered a violent fit of rage and had escaped from the hospital.

Police Commissioner Charles Warren. *Radio Times Hulton Picture Library*

Sir William Gull.

CENTRAL OFFICER'S
SPECIAL REPORT.

CRIMINAL INVESTIGATION DEPARTMENT,
SCOTLAND YARD,

17th day of November 1888

SUBJECT White chapel murders

REFERENCE TO PAPERS
5 2 983

Duly as reported
that an inquest was held
this day at the Shoreditch
Town Hall before Dr Macdonald
M. P. Coroner on the body of
Marie Jeanette Kelly, found
murdered at No. 13 Room,
Millers Court, Dorset Street,
Spitalfields. A number of
witnesses were called who
clearly established the
identity of deceased.
The Coroner remarked
that in his opinion it was
unnecessary to adjourn the
inquiry. and the jury returned
a verdict of "Wilful Murder
against some person or
persons unknown".
An important statement
has been made by a man
named George Hutchinson
which I forward herewith.
I have interrogated him
this evening and I am
of opinion his statement
(1) is

26,910 7 | 88 W. B. & Co.
891 5000 9 | 88 97,817

Metropolitan Police Officer's Special Report, November 12, 1888.

is true. He informed me
that he had occasionally
given the deceased a few
shillings, and that he
had known her about 3 years.
Also that he was surprised
to see a man so well
dressed in her company
which caused him to
watch them: He can identify
the man, and arrangement
was at once made for
two officers to accompany
him round the district for
a few hours tonight with
a view of finding the
man if possible.
Hutchinson is at present
in no regular employment,
and he has promised to
go with an officer tomorrow
morning at 11.30. am. to
the Shoreditch Mortuary to
identify the deceased.
Several arrests have
been made on suspicion
of

(2)

of being connected with
the recent murders, but
the various persons detained
have been able to satisfactorily
account for their movements
and were released.

F.G.Abberline, Supt

I. Arnold Supt.

(3)

Eddy on tour in India, January 1891. *Radio Times Hulton Picture Library*

"The Late Duke of Clarence Taking His Seat in the House of Lords" as Lord Salisbury looks on. *The Illustrated London News*, January 23, 1892. *Culver Pictures*

Eddy, in effigy, above his casket, while a weeping angel holds a kingly crown above his head. A crown he almost won!

Chapter 10

THE VENGEANCE

The predominant fact in Eddy's mind was that his father had once more betrayed him. His confinement at Balham was uninterrupted by news of his family, yet his father must have known that he was being kept there by Gull and Henry Acland. He wanted more than anything to tell James. James was the only friend he had, the one person he could trust.

But James did not know his whereabouts. This feeling that he had been isolated and completely put out of the way, coupled with his intense feelings of depression, proved unbearable.

He was the heir to the throne of England. His grandmother was the Queen, yet he had been treated as if he were a captive.

Physically he suffered from sudden shooting pains throughout his legs and arms and occasionally, when his eyes began to water, he could see nothing but darkness. It was the result of the drugs that he was given. In the mornings he vomited so violently that he could no longer taste food. He was positive that they were attempting to murder him, that his father did not care. He would be let die without a note or a visit.

Friday was his father's birthday. It would be celebrated at Sandringham with Georgie and his mother. He wanted to be there for that.

But first he had to see James and tell him everything. James would know what he should do.

He felt as if he were invisible again as he hurried toward Battersea Bridge. The distance to James's home in Kensington was less than a mile. It would still be dark when he arrived.

De Vere Gardens, which led from Canning Place into Kensington Road, was named after Aubrey De Vere and it, as well as all of Kensington, was once the property of the De Vere family, who subsequently became the Earls of Oxford. It looked out over Kensington Gardens, which were originally the private gardens of Kensington Palace, laid out in 1725 with beautiful avenues of trees and a small ornamental lake known as the Round Pond. The great elms which stood gracefully along the Broad Walk had provided a matchless setting for the Great Exhibition of 1851.

Victoria's husband, Prince Albert, had intended that this exhibition should surpass any in the history of the world, containing samples of what every country could produce in the way of raw materials, machinery, mechanical inventions, manufacture, and the applied arts. Albert had tried desperately to overcome the fact that he was a German living in a strange land, and Victoria had attempted to buoy his position by naming him (in 1857) Prince Consort. "The Queen has a right to claim that her husband should be an Englishman," she wrote. But Albert could not overcome the contradictions in his nature, the inner sickness which plagued him to become utterly severe, then gentle, modest, then scornful, longing for affection, and then cold and remote. So he drove himself to attain that perfection, mixed with sentimentality,* that plunged his entire family into a realm of shadowy longings intermingled with vague fears, of intense practicality which finally culminated in the uncontrollable madness of his namesake, Albert Victor.

* Although Christmas had long been a religious feast day celebrated by the English, Prince Albert had Teutonified the traditional British Christmas by introducing such sentimental German elements as the Christmas tree, which Dickens quickly popularized.

Both Prince Albert, the consort, and Albert Victor, the heir, were extremely unhappy men. Both were driven by ominous lacks in their nature to overcome this sense of depression. Both felt unloved and uncared for, and each experienced that mysterious Teutonic melancholy, that morbid appetite which plunged the one into tireless activity for "the good" and the other into incomprehensible dark rituals. One was "a saint," the other was a murderer. Both were trapped by a frigid, impregnable mass that they longed unsuccessfully to conquer.

On May 1, 1851, in a state of excitement bordering on delirium, Queen Victoria had opened the Great Exhibition in Kensington Gardens as a choir of six hundred voices burst into the "Hallelujah Chorus." She wrote later:

> It was the *greatest* day in our history, the most *beautiful* and *imposing* and *touching* spectacle ever seen, and the triumph of my beloved Albert . . .

James Stephen's home at 32 De Vere Gardens was located only a short walk from Victoria's memorial to Albert, the immense granite, white marble, and bronze gilt structure, with its one hundred and seventy life-size figures chiseled in a frieze. The monument had finally been completed in 1876 after twelve years of unrelenting toil and a cost of several hundred thousand pounds.

Except for the servants, James Stephen was alone in the house when Eddy arrived. He awakened and met Eddy in his dressing gown. It was barely light out and the most distressing thing that James noticed was Eddy's eyes. They were red and watery as if he had not slept in days.

James took him into the parlor and locked the parlor door. As soon as Eddy sat down, he burst into tears and began pouring out the story of his confinement. James listened in amazement as he went on, especially to the part involving Dr. Gull and Sir Henry Acland.

But Eddy's father must have known! The son of the Prince of Wales could not just disappear for weeks. But, Eddy went on, there was no visit from his father, not even a letter.

As Eddy continued with his story, James noticed that he

seemed extremely nervous, as if he expected at any moment to be found out, that someone might rush in, place him in chains, and forcibly take him back to Balham. No, James assured him, that would not happen. He was safe in his home.

Eddy told him of the shooting pains in his legs and arms, of his vomiting and sudden attacks when he was delirious and lost all sense of time. They were conspiring against him, he felt, and his father was at the back of it.

As he continued speaking, his voice grew weaker and the words slowly became less insistent, more drawn out, as though it required more of his concentration to speak than to think. There were lapses in his sentences and he was having more difficulty finding the words to express each thought, each feeling, until at last there was a long, inconclusive silence. At that moment, as James noticed the first light of day appearing in the windows overlooking Kensington Gardens, he turned to see that Eddy had fallen quietly to sleep.

When Dr. Gull learned of Eddy's escape, he quickly communicated with Sir Charles Warren. It was late morning before Sir Charles finally roused himself to pass on the information to Home Secretary Henry Matthews.

A small force of hand-picked men were detailed to the home of James Stephen located at 32 De Vere Gardens, as it was Gull's feeling that it was there the Prince would seek refuge.

James Stephen was awakened for the second time that morning, this time, by Sir Charles Warren, in person. James realized that there was no way he could hide Eddy in his house and he made no attempt to falsify the circumstances. He led Sir Charles and his officers to the parlor where he had left Eddy sleeping. However, when he opened the door, he saw that the room was empty.

After the police left his home, James checked the pantry to verify one of his servant's complaints that a long knife was missing.

Birthdays were sentimental times for the Prince of Wales. On Friday, November 9, he would be forty-seven and a celebration would be held at Sandringham with Alix, Georgie, and his daughters, Louise, Victoria, and Maud.

He had been informed by Dr. Gull that Eddy was suffering from syphilis and, as a result, was confined to a rest home for necessary treatment. Naturally, he had not conveyed this knowledge to his wife but had told her that Eddy had experienced a mild nervous breakdown and that both Dr. Gull and Henry Acland felt that he needed the time to himself in order fully to recover. Sadly, he remembered another birthday, nineteen years earlier, when Eddy had written that wonderfully innocent, childlike verse which he had read aloud at dinner:

> *Day of pleasure,*
> *Brightly dawning,*
> *Take the gift*
> *On this sweet morning.*
> *Our best hopes*
> *And wishes blending,*
> *Must yield joy*
> *That's never ending*

It was in Alix's handwriting but the sentiment behind it filled him with great pride. He had always hoped that his eldest son might overcome the terrible difficulties inherent in his nature. But as the years passed, seeing that Eddy was continuing in a state that seemed both unprogressive and hopeless, the Prince of Wales had turned his interest much more to Georgie. Though he was two years younger than his brother, Georgie had always seemed wiser and more mature. Forbidden childhood playmates, the Prince of Wales had longed for a pal as a son, and Georgie had fulfilled his expectations. He doted on the boy and had even confided to him in a letter of his love affair with the actress Lillie Langtry:

Yesterday we went to a morning performance at Haymarket Theatre and saw Goldsmith's comedy, *She Stoops to Conquer,* in which Mrs. Langtry acted with a professional company. It was her début, and a great success. As she is so very fond of acting, she has decided to go on the stage and will, after Christmas, join Mr. and Mrs. Bancroft's Company at the Haymarket.

Prince Jack

In this feeling for his younger son, the Prince of Wales regarded him almost as if he were his brother:

> On seeing you going off by the train yesterday, I felt very sad, and you could, I am sure, see that I had a lump in my throat when I wished you good-bye. We have been so much together, and especially lately, that I feel the parting doubly . . .

> On returning to Cannes to-day I shall miss you more than ever, my dear Georgie, and at the ball at Baroness Hoffman's—How I wish you could be at it!

The Prince of Wales could only experience great regret for Eddy. He loved him and wanted him to be cared for. Indeed, he would deeply miss his not being present at the birthday party on Friday.

Chapter 11

THE BIRTHDAY GIFT

The sink just off Dorset Street where Eddy had washed the blood from his hands on the morning of September 30, after his murder of Catherine Eddowes, was located only fifty yards from a two-story lodging house at No. 26, known as M'Carthy's Rents. The proprietor, John M'Carthy, who ran a small chandler's shop close by, had divided the original back parlor of the house into two separate rooms, the front one of which was designated Room 13. It was tiny, no more than twelve feet square, with a grated fireplace, a single bed, and its own entrance (the first door on the right) which led directly into a narrow passageway, about a yard and a half wide, known as Miller's Court. Farther up this passageway were six more cribs with whitewashed fronts, occupied mainly by prostitutes.

At the beginning of March 1888, John M'Carthy had let Room 13 for four shillings a week to an attractive twenty-four-year-old brunette named Marie Jeanette Kelly. She had striking blue eyes and a fresh, outdoor complexion which she had brought with her from Ireland. Tall and slightly buxom, she had a temper that sometimes got away from her, but it was the stories she told of herself, the fairy tales she concocted to compensate for the drabness of her life, which predominated in the minds of those who knew her.

Marie Jeanette was not even her real name, even though she often spoke of her well-to-do French parents and the fashionable brothel in which she once had lived in the West End. In truth, her actual name was Mary Jane Kelly, she was born in Limerick, and her parents were Irish Catholic.

When she was a child, her family had moved to Carmarthenshire, Wales, where her father, John Kelly, took a position as foreman in an ironworks. At the age of sixteen, she married a collier named Davies, but the marriage ended tragically a year later when Davies was killed in a mine explosion. The owners of the mine procrastinated for eighteen months before paying her a widow's pittance, and it was this delay which forced Mary Kelly onto the streets.

Heading for London, she roamed the notorious Ratcliffe Highway for a short time, then moved on to Stepney and Bethnal Green, before at last settling in the stews of Whitechapel. It was here that a young police constable named Walter Dew* first saw her. He was obviously somewhat smitten with her appearance, finding her, as he related afterward, "quite attractive." As he recalled:

> I knew Marie quite well by sight. Often I had seen her parading along Commercial Street, between Flower-and-Dean Street and Aldgate, or along Whitechapel Road. She was normally in the company of two or three of her kind, fairly neatly dressed and invariably wearing a clean white apron, but no hat.

Dorset Street,† off which Miller's Court led, was located directly across Commercial Street from Christ Church, Spitalfields. It was a rough, lawless neighborhood where meth drinkers and prostitutes abounded. Crimes committed along the street generally went unsolved as most members of the police force refused to venture up it without strong reinforcements.

* Dew was later to achieve fame as the man who arrested Dr. Crippen.
† Since named Duval Street.

Many of the prostitutes who lived there were young girls of four-teen and fifteen.‡ During the day they sat out on the sidewalk in front of the doss houses where they lived, while at night they solicited such pubs along Commercial Street as The Britannia, The Queen's Head, The Golden Hart, and The Ten Bells.

Marie Jeanette Kelly lived in Room 13 off Miller's Court with Joseph Barnett, who worked as a fish porter at Billingsgate. Some time in August, she had got herself pregnant by someone other than Barnett, and finally, on October 30 she and Barnett had a vi-olent row because she had brought home another prostitute whom she insisted on having share Room 13 with them both. The prostitute, a Mrs. Harvey, finally agreed to move to a lodging in New Court, but Marie and Barnett quarreled so violently that they broke the one window of her room, facing onto Dorset Street. Barnett stormed out, never to return. But his memory later was that Marie had an ominous, almost superstitious feeling about Jack the Ripper. "I used to buy newspapers and read her all the details of the Ripper murders," he recalled.

In actual fact, there was no woman in Whitechapel more frightened of Jack the Ripper than Marie Jeanette. Even though she looked forward enthusiastically to the spectacle which would take place on the morning of November 9, she had fearfully lamented to her nineteen-year-old friend Lizzie Albrook: "This will be the last Lord Mayor's Show I shall see. I can't stand it any longer. This Jack the Ripper business is getting on my nerves. I have made up my mind to go home to my mother. It is safer there."

After Barnett left, she had found herself desperate for money and had headed for the pubs along Commercial Street down to Leman Street and Aldgate to ply the trade she knew. She was six weeks behind in her rent and, prompted by the morning sickness as a result of her pregnancy and the turmoil with her lover, began to drink heavily. On the night of November 8, at eleven forty-five, her neighbor on Miller's Court, Mary Ann Cox, a widow who had also taken to prostitution, saw Marie Jeanette

‡ In 1881, a House of Lords Select Committee investigating child prostitution in London was told that in no other European city was it so prevalent.

emerging from The Britannia on the corner of Dorset and Commercial streets. The widow Cox noticed that Marie's hair, which she usually kept neatly pinned up, had fallen down around her shoulders and that she was drunk and reeling. With Marie was a stout, short man with a blotchy face and a full, red moustache. He was carrying a pail of beer in one hand, and he wore a round billycock hat. The widow Cox followed them to Miller's Court.

Marie bid a good night to Mary Ann Cox in front of the door to Room 13 and both she and the man disappeared inside. Mrs. Cox heard Marie's voice suddenly raised in a lilting burst of foolish playfulness: "Now I am going to have a song."

As Mrs. Cox proceeded up Miller's Court to her own squalid room, she heard Marie beginning a sentimental Irish ballad:

"Only a violet I plucked from my Mother's Grave . . ."

Fifteen minutes later, when she went out again, she could still hear Marie's voice:

"Zillah, darling one, I plucked it and brought it to you . . ."

The light was still on in Room 13.

When it began to rain at 1 A.M., Mrs. Cox returned once more to her room. Marie was still singing the same Irish ballad but Mrs. Cox noted that her voice seemed thin and tearful. Meanwhile, Eddy walked toward Whitechapel, carrying the black handbag which he had taken from the home of James Stephen. It contained a knife and two articles of women's clothing.

Sir William Gull's coachman helped the partially paralyzed physician into his carriage. Gull had communicated to Sir Charles Warren that he believed that Eddy, in the guise of Jack the Ripper, would strike again that night.

The rage that had infected the young man's personality would be directed at some tangible object, as an outlet, as it had been in the past. Although it was not Gull's realm to predict, since he had always dealt strictly with physical manifestations of diseases, he was positive now that the syphilis was only the more evident condition and that the real source of the Prince's violent acts went much deeper.

Understandably, Commissioner Warren had made no attempt

to alert the police or Scotland Yard, as Eddy's capture would have been difficult, if not impossible, to conceal. Consequently, Gull felt that the burden had fallen upon him. He would have to do whatever was possible to locate the Prince and to treat him as he would any other patient under his care.

It was a desperate situation, and yet he had no alternative but to circulate through Whitechapel. As his coach left the house at 74 Brook Street, Grosvenor Square, Gull wished that this nightmare might end. He must find the Prince before he committed a fifth murder.

The rain would not stop. The city's workmen had been called out to begin spreading gravel along the Victoria Embankment so as to prevent the horses' hoofs from slipping during the Lord Mayor's procession later that morning. Meanwhile, banners were being lettered with such slogans as *Honour and Probity* and *Labour Omnia Vincit*, as the Lord Mayor's coach, all gilt and golden with handpainted panels by Cipriani, stood ready for harnessing in Greenyard. It would be pulled by six horses, which had been borrowed from a local brewery, with six coachmen arrayed in scarlet and gold.

At 2 A.M., George Hutchinson, an unemployed night watchman, was wandering down Thrawl Street in the rain. He was without the money for a bed and his mood was one of utter depression. Just before reaching Flower-and-Dean Street, he met Marie Jeanette Kelly, who was walking alone. "Hutchinson, will you lend me sixpence?" she asked.

"I can't," he replied, "I have spent all my money going down to Romford."

Marie Jeanette shrugged, then added, "Good morning. I must go and find some money."

Hungrily, Hutchinson watched her as she moved off up Thrawl Street. In the past, he had once or twice taken her to the Cambridge Music Hall, where they sat in the fourpenny seats, and had bought her pink gins at The Britannia. But now, being without any employment for several weeks, his plight was even worse than hers. Yet he would have liked to have spent that rainy wet night with her in her bed.

He noticed a man coming from the opposite direction. Marie Jeanette stopped as the man tapped her on the shoulder and made some remark to her. Then they both burst out laughing.

Hutchinson was intrigued by the man's appearance. He seemed extremely well-dressed for the neighborhood, in his early thirties, above five feet eight inches tall, with a pale complexion, dark hair, and a slight moustache curled up at each end. He also had a parcel in his hand with a strap around it. Hutchinson heard Marie agree, "All right," and the man add, "*You* will be all right for what I have told you." The man put his arm around Marie's shoulders and guided her down the street toward Hutchinson, who now stood in front of The Queen's Head pub. As they passed by him, the man kept his head down and his felt hat over his eyes.

More intrigued than ever, Hutchinson followed them to Dorset Street, where they stopped at the entrance to Miller's Court. The man said something that Hutchinson could not make out and then Marie replied, quite clearly, "All right, my dear. Come along, you will be comfortable." He then placed his hand again on her shoulder as she murmured something about having lost her handkerchief. The man pulled out his, a red one, before they started up the court. Hutchinson walked somberly away, assuming that they had both already entered Room 13.

There is no way to describe what actually occurred in that room. The frenzy that overcame Eddy and the violence which he enacted upon Marie Jeanette Kelly occupied the next two hours. At its conclusion, Eddy burned his clothes, which were saturated with blood, in the grated fireplace by the bed. He then dressed himself in a woman's dress and shawl which he had brought with him in the black handbag.

Shortly after 4 A.M., he escaped through the muslin-curtained window, still broken from the quarrel between Marie and her lover, Joseph Barnett, the week before.

Chapter 12

THE CELEBRATION

At 10 A.M., the guns which began to boom from the Tower of London were echoed by roaring volleys from the Horse Guards Parade in royal salute to the Prince of Wales. "Dear Bertie's birthday," Queen Victoria noted in her diary under the date, November 9, 1888. "May God bless him," she added, "he has a warm affectionate heart and is a very dutiful and good son." The years had mellowed her opinion of the now middle-aged man about whom she had written twenty-five years before: "Oh, how different *poor foolish* Bertie is to adored Papa, whose gentle, loving, wise and motherly care of me, when he was not 21, exceeded everything!"

At ten-thirty in an antechamber of Mansion House, Lord Mayor-elect James Whitehead put on the scarlet gown lined with white silk and trimmed with sable which he would wear in the parade beginning at noon. In his right hand, he held the crystal mace which dated from the days of the Anglo-Saxon rulers. Soon he would also hold the gold purse which would be ceremoniously handed to him, as it had been handed to each new Lord Mayor since the reign of Elizabeth I.

At ten forty-five, John M'Carthy noted that Marie Jeanette Kelly was six weeks behind in her rent. He had been put off by her promises and tales of woe week after week, until now the sum due totaled twenty-nine shillings.

"Bowyer," he called to his assistant, "go around to 13 Miller's Court and get what you can from the Kelly woman on the rent she owes us."

Five minutes later, the cannons were still roaring their birthday greeting to the Prince of Wales when Harry Bowyer pounded on the door of Room 13. Getting no response, he tried the door handle. It would not budge. Going around to the side, he poked his hand through the broken pane of glass and pulled back the muslin curtain inside. He was suddenly chilled to the bone by what he saw.

He backed away, shaken for an instant, before finally forcing himself to look again. Then he hurriedly turned and rushed back to tell M'Carthy of his discovery.

"Great God, Harry, do you mean that!" M'Carthy roared as he raced back with him to the room. But the sight was even more ghastly than Bowyer had described. Quickly sending his assistant to the police station for help, M'Carthy waited for several minutes on the street in front of the room.

Bowyer arrived back with Inspector Beck and Walter Dew, the young police constable who, from a distance, had long admired Marie Jeanette Kelly. When Bowyer pointed to the room, Dew tried the door, but it would not yield. Meanwhile, Inspector Beck pushed back the curtain and peered through the aperture in the window. A moment later, he staggered back, his face white as a sheet.

"For God's sake, Dew," he cried. "Don't look."

Ignoring the order, Dew stared through the window. As his eyes became accustomed to the dim light, he saw a sight which would remain with him as the most gruesome memory of his whole police career. There was a table just beneath the window. On the bed, which was drawn obliquely across the small room, was all that remained of the pretty, buxom young woman he had often observed parading along Commercial Street and White-chapel Road. There was little left of her, not much more than a skeleton. Her face was horribly mutilated. But the sight which would remain most vividly with Constable Dew was Marie Kelly's eyes. They were wide open and staring at him in terror.

Inspector Beck had quickly recovered from his shock and had ordered a telegram rushed to Divisional Superintendent Arnold telling him what had happened. Obviously nothing could be done for the victim, but Dr. George Bagster Phillips was sent for as a matter of form.

Within minutes, Inspector Frederick Abberline arrived. He was a portly and gentle-speaking man who could have been taken for the manager of a bank or a solicitor. He was extremely familiar with crime and criminals in the East End, as for many years he had been Detective Inspector of the Whitechapel Division, or, as he was then called, the "Local Inspector." He gave orders to seal off the Court. Nobody was to enter or leave without his permission. He also refused to let anyone enter Room 13 until Commissioner Warren's bloodhounds could show what they could do.

Sir Charles Warren had devoted all his energies to preventing the riot of Socialists which had been planned to disrupt the Lord Mayor's Parade. He had issued the strictest orders that:

> No person, unless forming part of the Lord Mayor's procession, shall be allowed to deliver any public speech, or to carry placards or banners, in any street or thoroughfare through which the Lord Mayor's procession passes.

Scores of mounted police were detailed to reinforce the City police along the parade route, while Trafalgar Square was manned with every available officer he could find.

Following the news of Eddy's escape from Balham's House of Rest, Warren had attempted to center all focus on the Lord Mayor's show, and, even though the so-called "Socialist riot" was solely his own invention it served to deploy the detective staff of

Scotland Yard away from the area where the Prince might be captured.

At no time had he the intention of using bloodhounds, and when he learned that Inspector Abberline was awaiting their arrival at the scene of the murder in Miller's Court, he reacted by completely ignoring Abberline's request.

At 1 P.M., when the Lord Mayor's procession turned into Fleet Street from Ludgate Circus beside St. Paul's Cathedral, newsboys appeared with placards, waving and screaming:

MURDER—ANOTHER MURDER—JACK THE RIPPER—LATEST VICTIM!

Pandemonium broke loose. Spectators snatched the placards and held them up to the faces of the marching police, jeering, "Yah, look at this!" A score of medical students rushed down Ludgate Hill knocking down pedestrians as their leader jumped onto the back of a police constable, hurling him to the ground. Fists and billyclubs flew as dozens of arrests were made. One young man was carried face down to the nearest station house, while the new Lord Mayor, Sir James Whitehead, was cast into the background. Jack the Ripper had once more stolen the show. "The murderer chose his time well," The *Star* commented. "He got his sensation."

Superintendent Arnold could wait no longer for Commissioner Warren and his bloodhounds. It was one forty-five and the ghoulish sightseers crowding into Dorset Street had reached the emergency state. The room had to be broken into.

Once again, Police Constable Walter Dew, who still had not left the murder scene, was one of the first to enter the room. As Dew recalled:

The sight that confronted us was indescribable, infinitely more horrifying than what I had seen peering through the broken pane of glass. I had seen the remains of most of the other Ripper victims. But none of the others approached for bestial brutality the treatment of the body of poor Marie . . . There was no fire in the grate, but there were signs that there had been a big blaze. For one thing the kettle standing on the burnt-out fire had melted at the spout. Candles which had been used to light the room had been burned right down. The girl's clothing had nearly all been cut from her body in the process of mutilation. All these things I saw after I had slipped and fallen on the awfulness of that floor.

Prior to 1830, London did not have an effective police force. When, in 1750, Justice of the Peace Henry Fielding (who in 1749 had published his novel *Tom Jones*) managed to convince the Home Secretary that London could not combat the rising tide of crime without some sort of police, he was granted money for an unofficial organization named after his court in Bow Street: the Bow Street Runners. There were fifteen of them, each paid a guinea a day, to combat the approximately thirty thousand thieves operating in the city.

Englishmen had long considered police a threat to their liberty, maintaining that it was the business of the individual to maintain order and guard property. But finally, in 1829, Home Secretary Robert Peel, after a bitter struggle in the House of Commons, managed to set up an official police force. Numbering a thousand policemen, in long blue coats and black hats, they paraded through the streets to their new stations. "Bobbies," they were jeeringly called, and the name stuck.

Several brutal murders in 1842 prompted twelve men, with headquarters in Scotland Yard, to take off their uniforms and become detectives, but they were greeted with extreme distrust. In 1869, Police Commissioner Edmund Henderson reported that a detective force was "entirely foreign to the habits and feelings of the nation." But in the early 1870s, the methods of the Sûreté in Paris were becoming well known and an English lawyer, Howard Vincent, set up the Criminal Investigation Department—the C.I.D.—to be modeled after the French unit.

The great turning point in English criminal detection almost came in 1880, when a Scottish physician, Henry Faulds, wrote to the London weekly *Nature*:

In looking over some specimens of prehistoric pottery found in Japan, I noticed certain finger marks which had been made on them while the clay was still soft. A comparison of such fingertip impressions made in recent pottery led me to observe the character of the skin furrows in human fingers generally.

Faulds had begun to collect and classify numerous fingerprints when a thief climbed over a whitewashed wall near where he lived and impressions of his sooty fingertips were left on the wall. Learning that a suspect had been arrested, he asked the Japanese police to take the prisoner's fingerprints. As they were different from those left on the wall, Faulds insisted that the man was innocent. A few days later, when the actual thief was found, the fingerprints matched. Faulds then proposed a revolutionary idea: What if the police were to look for fingerprints at the scene of *every* crime? He wrote to the Home Secretary and the London Police Commissioner, but his suggestion was ignored.

In the spring of 1888, Faulds's theory was championed by Francis Galton, the cousin of Charles Darwin. Galton was convinced that fingerprints could be classified into four basic patterns. The key factor was a triangular formation, a "delta" which occurred in almost every print. It might be on the left or right side of the finger; while some fingers had more than one "delta," others had none at all.

Unfortunately, Galton was a little too late for Jack the Ripper. The one detective on duty that day in Miller's Court who came closest to applying some theory of modern police detection was Assistant Police Commissioner Henry Smith. He ordered that both the body and the room be photographed.*

At three forty-five, Marie Kelly's cloth-covered remains were transported from Room 13 in a scratched, dirty coffin before the eyes of hundreds of horrified spectators. A few moments later the windows of her room were sealed with wooden planks, the door was padlocked, and a policeman was stationed in front to keep away sightseers.

Windsor Castle had long been regarded as the home of the British monarchy. But after Prince Albert's death, Victoria's con-

---

* Unfortunately, these photographs were later "misplaced," or purposely lost, by Assistant Police Commissioner Smith's superiors.

tinued mourning filled the atmosphere with such somberness that the Prince of Wales finally had to move his family to Sandringham, the seven-thousand-acre estate he had purchased shortly before his marriage. Here, away from the brooding, grief-stricken Queen, he indulged his passion for hunting and often personally led his guests on tours of the stables, the kennels, the gardens, and the stud farm where he raised race horses. Windsor was visited only during Easter and Ascot Week, while Sandringham, located less than two hours from London by train, was where the Prince of Wales, his wife, Alexandra, and their children gathered as a family.

When Eddy arrived at Sandringham on November 9 to attend his father's birthday, he explained the reason for his wearing a woman's dress and shawl was that he had attended a costume party the night before. He privately joked that he had gone to the affair dressed as his grandmother.

His father knew, however, that Eddy had escaped from the rest home at Balham. He had already been informed of this by Henry Acland.

On the surface, it began as a warm family reunion. However, shortly after luncheon, a telegram arrived that Eddy would have to return to London. Both Henry Acland and Dr. Gull were awaiting him at Gull's house in Grosvenor Square. The Prince of Wales bid his son farewell and sent him back by coach.

Within hours after the discovery of the murder in Miller's Court, Commissioner Charles Warren met with Home Secretary Henry Matthews. Both men were desperate. The public clamor arising from this latest brutal murder might not only force the discovery of the killer's identity, but it could, as well, reveal their roles as accomplices.

Matthews had already met with Lord Salisbury, who was shaken by the prospects. There seemed to be no alternative but for Warren to resign as Commissioner of Police. In his place, Matthews would appoint James Monro, the former head of the C.I.D. Monro, who had already been apprised of the situation, had agreed to cooperate with the Government in protecting the identity of the murderer.

It was a bitter pill for Sir Charles Warren to swallow. Monro, when he was head of the C.I.D., had already caused Warren great embarrassment by refusing to answer to him. Monro had looked down on Warren from the beginning and, even though by rank he was only an Assistant Commissioner, he chose to report solely to Home Secretary Matthews, overlooking both Warren's superior rank and his position as Metropolitan Police Commissioner. Finally, in August 1888, Warren had forced Monro to resign, appointing to the post Sir Robert Anderson. Now, in a matter of only three months, Monro had succeeded in replacing Warren as Police Commissioner.

But Warren's only recourse was to go along with Matthews' plan. He would tender his written resignation, which would be back-dated November 8, *the day prior to the Miller's Court murder*. It was also agreed that he would issue, at his last official act, a pardon for himself and for all those who were aware of the killer's identity. That afternoon, an official notice was posted in every police station in London with Sir Charles Warren's signature:

> MURDER—PARDON. Whereas on November 8 or 9 in Miller's Court, Dorset Street, Spitalfields, Mary Jane Kelly was murdered by some person or persons unknown, the Secretary of State will advise the grant of Her Majesty's pardon to any accomplice not being a person who contrived or actually committed the murder who shall give such information and evidence as shall lead to the discovery and conviction of the person or persons who committed the murder.

Ironically, if, in fact, Warren had officially resigned on November 8, how could the pardon signed by him be considered binding since it was issued *after*, and *as a result of*, the discovery of Marie Jeanette Kelly's body *on November 9*?

Chapter 13

THE MEDIUM

Robert James Lees, since turning down Victoria's offer to act as the spiritualist link between her and her dear deceased Albert, had devoted his energies to exploring the world of the psyche and preparing his first book on the subject, *Through the Mists*. Throughout the year 1888, he had been experimenting at the Spiritualist Center in Peckham, where he conducted séances and exercises in clairvoyancy. While there, he reportedly *saw* Jack the Ripper.

Lees was writing in his study when he experienced the sensation that the Ripper was about to commit another murder. That night in a dream he saw two persons, a man and a woman, walking down a dimly lighted street. He followed them in his mind's eye down a narrow passageway into what appeared as a courtyard. He watched as they entered a dark corner of the yard. The woman was half-drunk; the man was perfectly sober. The man put his hand over the woman's mouth. She struggled, but was too overcome by liquor to make any effectual resistance. The man then drew a knife and cut the woman's throat.

When Lees awakened the following morning, he found the

dream written down on a pad beside his bed, though he had no recollection of writing it.

Lees was so overcome by the violence of his vision that he went that day to Scotland Yard and related the dream in detail to the detectives there. They regarded him as one more lunatic, so inundated were they by hundreds of cranks with "Jack the Ripper" theories.

Lees was completely shaken the following morning, September 8, when Annie Chapman's body was discovered in the backyard of No. 29 Hanbury Street. Taking with him an assistant, he visited the scene of the murder, joining the throng of sightseers streaming in off Commercial Road. The fenced-in yard behind No. 29 Hanbury Street turned out to be the courtyard he had envisioned in his dream. Lees recalled:

> I felt almost as if I were an accessory before the fact. It made such an impression on me that my whole nervous system was seriously shaken. I could not sleep at night and under the advice of a physician I removed with my family to the Continent.

During his visit abroad, he no longer was troubled by his strange visions of the killer at work. But finally it became necessary for him to return home to London.

On the afternoon of November 9, while riding in an omnibus, he saw a man enter a house in the fashionable Grosvenor Square area. Leaning over to his wife, he remarked intently, "That is Jack the Ripper." His wife laughed at him, telling him not to be foolish. "I am not mistaken," Lees replied. "I feel it."

Lees quickly got off the bus and found a constable. He related to him that he had just seen Jack the Ripper enter the house at 74 Brook Street. The constable laughed at him, threatening to "run him in." Lees hastened to Scotland Yard where he found an inspector who was willing to accompany him to 74 Brook Street the following morning. There the inspector balked at the entrance to the house, as it was the residence of one of the West End's most celebrated physicians, Sir William Gull. He finally challenged Lees to describe the interior of the house. "The hall has a high porter's chair of black oak on the right hand as you enter it," Lees began. "There is a stained-glass window at the extreme end, and a large mastiff is at this moment asleep at the foot of the stairs."

Lees and the inspector waited until seven o'clock, when the servants would be up and around, before knocking on the front door. The servant who let them in informed them that Dr. Gull was still sleeping but that they might speak with his wife. As they entered the front hall, which was exactly as Lees had described, he noticed that there was no mastiff by the stairs. Questioning the servant as to the dog's whereabouts, Lees learned that it generally slept at the foot of the stairs but it was let out into the back garden every morning.

Mrs. Gull with her daughter Caroline* came down the stairs, and Lees began to interrogate her. After a few moments, Dr. Gull appeared. Under Lees's barrage of questions, Gull explained that since his stroke in 1887 he had suffered losses of memory and on one occasion had found blood on his shirt.

There was nothing that could be done, however, as Gull was not the man Lees had seen enter the house, and Gull insisted that neither he nor his family had any knowledge who that person was.

Lees later claimed that he received payments from the Privy Purse to keep silent. Like so many others, records of these payments have disappeared.

Marie Kelly's inquest began on Monday morning, November 12, after Lord Salisbury summoned his cabinet members to an emergency meeting at No. 10 Downing Street. It was decided that the inquest proceedings should be hushed up. In order to assure this, Wynne R. Baxter, the coroner who had presided at the inquests of Polly Nicholls, Annie Chapman, Elizabeth Stride, and Catherine Eddowes, and the first person who had challenged the police and the Government's attempts to stifle and confuse the testimony of these hearings, had to be replaced. It was Salisbury's decision that the inquest should be conducted by Dr. Roderick MacDonald, a Member of Parliament, who could be counted on

---

* Dr. Gull's daughter, who became Lady Caroline Acland in the 1930s, recounted to Dr. Thomas Stowell the visit by Lees to her parents' home and her father's attempt to shield Eddy.

to go along with the position of both the Government and the police.

London's daily newspapers heatedly attacked the switch of coroners. But Dr. MacDonald calmly fielded all questions thrust upon him by anxious reporters. It seemed incredible to them that Marie Jeanette Kelly's body, which had been found mutilated and murdered in Whitechapel, should have been moved to an entirely separate district for the inquest. MacDonald replied that he had had absolutely *no communication at all* with Whitechapel Coroner Wynne R. Baxter. "The body is in my jurisdiction," he coolly added. "It was taken to my mortuary, and that is the end of the matter."

But the furor would not subside. On Monday morning at the start of the inquest proceedings, one of the jurors lashed out at MacDonald: "I do not see why we should have the inquest thrown on our shoulders when the murder did not happen in our district, *but in Whitechapel*."

Mr. Hammond, the Coroner's officer, quickly interceded: "It did *not* happen in Whitechapel."

His comment, of course, was utterly false, and MacDonald quickly had to take hold of the situation by angrily castigating the questioning juror: "Do you think that we do not know what we are doing here? The jury are summoned in the ordinary way, and they have no business to object. If they persist in their objection I shall know how to deal with them. Does any juror persist in objecting?"

Suppression of the truth now appeared blatant, but the juror refused to back down: "We are summoned for the Shoreditch district. This affair happened in Spitalfields."

MacDonald coldly slammed back at him: "It happened within my district."

Immediately another aroused juror chimed in: "This is not my district. I come from Whitechapel, and Mr. Baxter is my coroner."

MacDonald, at this point, shrugged both of them off: "I am not going to discuss the subject with the jurymen at all. If any juryman says he distinctly objects, let him say so." Hesitating a moment, MacDonald quickly added: "I may tell the jurymen that jurisdiction lies where the body lies, not where it was found."

In the face of this preposterous bit of logic, the jurors were sworn in, but before any evidence was given, they were taken by Inspector Abberline to the mortuary to view the body, which was still lying in its battered coffinshell. A soiled gray sheet covered the body up to the neck, so that the mutilations mercifully could not be seen. The face was carved and disfigured beyond recognition. Only the eyes showed any signs of humanity. According to the *Pall Mall Gazette*, it resembled "one of those horrible wax anatomical specimens."

The jurors were then taken to inspect the boarded-up room in Miller's Court, before returning to Shoreditch Town Hall for testimony.

The first witness was Joseph Barnett, the Billingsgate fish porter who had lived with Marie Jeanette Kelly just prior to her murder. He was followed by: Thomas Bowyer, the rent collector, who had discovered the body; John M'Carthy, the landlord of No. 13 Miller's Court; Mary Ann Cox, Marie Jeanette's neighbor, and various other prostitutes who lived in the neighborhood and had either known or seen Marie Kelly prior to her murder. Finally, Dr. George Bagster Phillips read briefly from his medical report, but was not allowed to go into detail concerning the wounds inflicted. With that, Dr. MacDonald abruptly ended the hearing, without even attempting to establish the nature of the murder weapon. He recorded the jury's verdict: "willful murder against some person or persons unknown," over the astonishment of both the jurors and the spectators. "There is other evidence which I do not propose to call," he then announced grandly, "for if we at once make public every fact brought forward in connection with this terrible murder the ends of justice might be retarded."

It was an extraordinary statement. Especially since the one witness that he had purposely neglected to call was George Hutchinson, the market porter who had followed Marie Jeanette Kelly and Eddy back to the room off Miller's Court on that terrible morning of November 9.

But Hutchinson would never be allowed to testify or to

describe publicly the murderer. Instead, as Inspector Abberline reported: "Arrangement was at once made for two officers to accompany him round the district for a few hours tonight with a view of finding the man if possible." Abberline's report was dated November 12, the day of MacDonald's abruptly terminated inquest, and it continues: "Hutchinson is at present in no regular employment, and he has promised to go with an officer tomorrow morning at 11:30 A.M. to the Shoreditch Mortuary to identify the deceased." There is no account of Hutchinson's reaction when he first viewed Marie Jeanette's mutilated remains. No further attempt was made to use him to identify the man he saw with her, although as Abberline reported, Hutchinson had been "surprised to see a man so well dressed in her company which caused him to watch them. *He can identify the man.*"

But the most overt attempt to sidetract any clarifying details which might have slipped into the public's consciousness from the inquest was the appointment of a second physician to perform a post-mortem on the body of Marie Jeanette Kelly. Dr. Thomas Bond was Police Divisional Surgeon and thus could be trusted to safeguard the interests of his superiors. Of all the post-mortems conducted on the various murder victims, his report is the only one included in the official Ripper file:

7 THE SANCTUARY
WESTMINSTER ABBEY
November 10th, 1888

Dear Sir,
   Whitechapel Murders
   I beg to report that I have read the notes of the four Whitechapel Murders viz:—
   1. Buck's Row
   2. Hanbury Street
   3. Berner Street
   4. Mitre Square
I have also made a Post-Mortem Examination of the mutilated remains of a woman found yesterday in a small room in Dorset Street:—
   1.   All five murders were no doubt committed by the same hand. In the first four the throats appear to have been cut

from left to right, in the last case owing to the extensive mutilation it is impossible to say in what direction the fatal cut was made, but arterial blood was found on the wall in splashes close to where the woman's head must have been lying.

2.   All the circumstances surrounding the murders lead me to form the opinion that the women must have been lying down when murdered and in every case the throat was first cut.

3.   In the four murders of which I have seen the notes only, I cannot form a very definite opinion as to the time that had elapsed between the murder and the discovery of the body. In one case, that of Berner Street, the discovery appears to have been immediately after the deed. In Buck's Row, Hanbury Street and Mitre Square three or four hours only could have elapsed. In the Dorset Street case the body was lying on the bed at the time of my visit at two o'clock quite naked and mutilated as in the annexed report. Rigor Mortis had set in but increased during the progress of the examination. From this it is difficult to say with any degree of certainty the exact time that had elapsed since death as the period varies from six to twelve hours before rigidity sets in. The body was comparatively cold at two o'clock and the remains of a recently taken meal were found in the stomach and scattered about over the intestines. It is, therefore, pretty certain that the woman must have been dead about twelve hours and the partly digested food would indicate that death took place about three or four hours after food was taken in, so one or two o'clock in the morning would be the probable time of the murder.

4.   In all the cases there appears to be no evidence of struggling and the attacks were probably so sudden and made in a position that the women could neither resist nor cry out. In the Dorset St. case the corner of the sheet to the right of the woman's head was much cut and saturated with blood, indicating that the face may have been covered with the sheet at the time of the attack.

5.   In the first four cases the murderer must have attacked from the right side of the victim. In the Dorset Street case, he must have attacked from in front or from the left, as there would be no room for him between the wall and the

147

part of the bed on which the woman was lying. Again the blood had flowed down on the right side of the woman and spurted on to the wall.

6.   The murderer would not necessarily be splashed or deluged with blood, but his hands and arms must have been covered and parts of his clothing must certainly have been smeared with blood.

7.   The mutilations in each case excepting the Berner Street one were all of the same character and showed clearly that in all the murders the object was mutilation.

8.   In each case the mutilation was implicated by a person who had no scientific nor anatomical knowledge. In my opinion he does not even possess the technical knowledge of butcher or horse slaughterman or any person accustomed to cut up dead animals.

9.   The instrument must have been a strong knife at least six inches long, very sharp, pointed at the top and about an inch in width. It may have been a clasp knife, a butcher's knife or a surgeon's knife. I think it was no doubt a straight knife.

10. The murderer must have been a man of physical strength and of great coolness and daring. There is no evidence that he had an accomplice. He must in my opinion be a man subject to periodical attacks of Homicidal and Erotic mania. The character of the mutilations indicate that the man may be in a condition sexually, that may be called Satyriasis. It is of course possible that the Homicidal impulse may have developed from a revengeful or brooding condition of the mind, or that religious mania may have been the original disease but I do not think either hypothesis is likely. The murderer in external appearance is quite likely to be a quiet inoffensive looking man probably middle-aged† and neatly and respectably dressed. I think he must be in the habit of wearing a cloak or overcoat or he could hardly have escaped notice in the streets if the blood on his hands or clothes were visible.

11. Assuming the murderer to be such a person as I have just described, he would be solitary and eccentric in his habits, also he is most likely to be a man without regular occupa-

† Dr. Bond's unsubstantiated assumption that the murderer was "middle-aged" when two witnesses had already described him as being in his late twenties was obviously intended to avert suspicion from the actual person.

tion, but with some small income‡ or pension. He is possibly living among respectable persons who have some knowledge of his character and habits and who may have grounds for suspicion that he isn't quite right in his mind at times. Such persons would probably be unwilling to communicate suspicions to the Police for fear of trouble or notoriety, whereas if there were prospect of reward it might overcome their scruples.

On Sunday, November 18, at noon, the funeral began. The crowd which gathered in front of St. Leonard's Church, Shoreditch, was composed mostly of women who, as the *East London Advertiser* reported, "struggled desperately to get to touch the coffin. Women with faces streaming with tears cried out, 'God forgive her' and every man's head was bared in token of sympathy." On the coffin plate was engraved:

Marie Jeanette Kelly, died 9th November, 1888, aged 25.

It was 2 P.M. when the mourners, who included Joseph Barnett, the Billingsgate fish porter, reached St. Patrick's Catholic Cemetery at Leytonstone. The burial service took only a few minutes and later Harry Wilson, the clerk of St. Leonard's Church, who had paid the costs for the funeral, announced that if the public wished to share in the cost of erecting a tombstone, their contributions would be welcome. No tombstone was ever erected.

On the Sunday morning following Marie Jeanette Kelly's murder, a man with a face blackened by burnt cork with huge rings of white painted around his eyes stood on the corner of Wentworth and Commercial streets wailing, "I am Jack the Ripper!" He was seized by two men as a mob armed with raised sticks and clubs surged upon him with the chilling cry: "Lynch him!" He might have been lynched on the spot except for the immediate arrival of four constables from the Leman Street Station, who dragged him through the crowded streets to the station

‡ Taking into account Dr. Bond's obvious purpose, to obscure the real identity of the murderer, it is understandable that he was unable to make the mental leap to imagine a man with *some great income*.

house where he reluctantly admitted that he was a doctor at St. George's Hospital, Hyde Park Corner, but refused to give his name.

Three weeks later, his corpse reportedly was dredged up from the Thames by the River Police, near Hungerford Bridge. A paddle boat tied to the Waterloo Pier had shifted, causing the black swollen body to come to the surface, for it had been imbedded under the wheel. According to Edwin T. Woodhall's account, "The black burnt cork and white paint on the already decomposing features were hideously evident."

This incident was to hold eerie overtones for the circumstances which were about to unfold. It would serve once again to avert the public's suspicions from the actual identity of the killer, but the curious result was that it clouded the minds of so many intelligent individuals who for the last eighty years have had the killer's identity staring them in the face and yet have been unwilling or unable to admit its presence.

From Balmoral Castle in Scotland, Queen Victoria, after hearing of Marie Jeanette Kelly's murder, had charged Lord Salisbury:

> This new most ghastly murder shows the absolute necessity for some decided action. All these courts must be lit, and our detectives improved. They are not what they should be.

Despite Victoria's plea, in the weeks following, senior inspectors and constables assigned to Whitechapel were quietly withdrawn *en masse*. It was as if the police were unusually confident that there would be no more murders.

Albert Backert, a member of the Whitechapel Vigilance Committee, was alarmed by Scotland Yard's sudden complacency and was aroused enough to want to know why. He went personally to police headquarters and demanded an interview:

> I was asked if I would agree to be sworn to secrecy, on the understanding that I was given certain information. Foolishly, I agreed. It was then suggested to me that the Vigilance Committee and its patrols might be disbanded *as the police were quite certain that the Ripper was dead*. I protested that, as I had been sworn to secrecy, I really ought to be given more information than this.

"It isn't necessary for you to know any more," I was told. "The man in question is dead. *He was fished out of the Thames two months ago* and it would only cause pain to relatives if we said any more than that."

I again protested that I had been sworn to secrecy for nothing, that I was really no wiser than before. "If there are no murders, I shall respect this confidence, but if there are any more I shall consider that I am absolved from my pledge of secrecy." The police then got very tough. They told me a pledge was a solemn matter, that *anyone who put out stories that the Ripper was still alive might be proceeded against for causing a public mischief.*

Lord Salisbury's planned deception now appeared flawless. There seemed to be no avenue through which the murderer's identity could be uncovered. The net of secrecy would hold as long as Eddy was continually confined and treated by Dr. Gull through drugs and hypnotic suggestion. Yet what would happen if Eddy should escape once more, and commit a sixth murder?

Chapter 14

ALEXANDRA

Princess Alexandra was extremely protective of her youngest son, George, and as he was growing up, she had written to him continuously. In contrast, she hardly ever wrote to Eddy, although he wrote her countless letters. However, shortly after the Prince of Wales had been nursed back to health by Doctor Gull, following his typhoid attack in 1871, she had written a note to her eldest son that was so cloyingly sweet that even at the age of eight Eddy must have felt terrifyingly removed from his mother. Yet it was one of the only letters he was ever to receive from her:

> My own darling little Eddy,
> Mama sends a thousand thanks for all the very nice little letters, and is so glad to hear from Mr. Dalton that Eddy is a good little boy. Mama is so glad dear little Eddy has been going on praying God for dear Papa's recovery and the Almighty God has *heard* our prayers, and darling Papa is going to be quite well again and very soon we hope you may all come home again to see dear Papa once more! Mama is so glad her little chicks will spend a happy and merry Christmas with dear Grandmama, and Mama sends

you each a little Christmas card with many good wishes for
Christmas and the New Year, which I hope will begin brightly
and happily for all of us, and that my little Eddy will try and become a very good obedient boy. Remember me kindly to Mr. Dalton with many thanks for all his letters, kiss Grandma's hand,
and give my love to Uncle Leo and Aunt Beatrice.

> Ever you loving,
> Mama Alix

Alexandra treated Eddy always as a child, an awkward unfortunate child, whose inner turmoil she attributed, as she once admitted to her mother-in-law, the Queen, to "having grown so fast."

In contrast, George, who was two years younger than Eddy, was
"the man" in her eyes, and in her love letters to him it was obvious that he was the masculine object of her lonely affections:

My own darling little Georgie,
I have only just left you going to bed, after having given you my
last kiss and having heard you say your prayers. I need hardly say
what I feel—and what we both feel at this sad hour of parting—
It will be harder for you this time to have to go quite by yourself
—without Eddy, Mr. Dalton or Fuller—but remember darling
that when all others are far away God is always there—and He
will never forsake you—but bring you safe back to all of us who
love you so—
I need hardly say my darling Georgie *how* much I shall always
miss you—now we have been so much together and you were
such a dear little boy not at all spoilt and so nice and affectionate
to old Motherdear—Remain just as you are—but strive to get on
in all that is good—and keep out of temptation as much as you
can—dont let anyone lead you astray—Remember to take the
Sacrament about every quarter which will give you fresh strength
to do what is right—and also never forget either your morning or
your evening Prayer—We must all try and console ourselves by
thinking how quickly the year will pass and what delight it will be
to meet once more . . . And now darling Georgie I must say
Goodnight and Goodbye as I am so sleepy my eyes will hardly
keep awake and it is nearly two—so goodbye and God bless you
and keep you safe and sound till we meet again and watch over
you wherever you are—
Goodbye, goodbye, Georgie dear

153

With a father who was embarrassed by him and a mother whose affections were centered on his younger brother, the predominant figure in Eddy's life had been his tutor, Reverend Dalton. Gradually he grew to despise Dalton, and there was good reason. It was Dalton who had continually complained to the Prince of Wales of Eddy's "weakness of brain, the feebleness and lack of power to grasp anything put before him," and had further branded Eddy's condition as "a fault of nature." But Dalton dealt him a final blow by letting Alexandra know of Eddy's animosity toward him, to which she replied in an attempt to assuage the tutor's feelings:

> Although you kindly beg me not to distress myself about the contents of your last letter I cannot, I confess, help being very much grieved by the unsatisfactory account you are unfortunately obliged to give me of Eddy! It is indeed a bitter disappointment that instead of steadily improving himself as we hoped he had begun to do during the first half of his stay at Lausanne he should have relapsed into his old habits of indolence and inattention. It does indeed seem strange that at his age* he does not yet see the great importance of exerting himself to the utmost, and lets his precious time slip by which can never be recalled.
>
> But what pains me more than all this is his *seeming* ingratitude towards you, who, although you have always taken so humble and unselfish a view of your own services, have really devoted the best years of your life for his welfare and have thought no trouble too great as long as it could conduce to the good of the boys. Believe me, although I can so well understand how disheartening it appears to you at this moment, that Eddy is *not* so insensible as you think to all the good and devotion he owes to you and that all the trouble you take is only *for his own sake and as a true friend* towards him. At any rate I feel sure he will some day appreciate at its proper value all the sacrifices you have made on his behalf.

Although Alexandra occasionally forced herself to recognize Eddy's mental derangement, she was never conscious of its extent. Most of her life was fantasy, prompted by the bitter relationship she shared with her husband. Whenever possible she tried to idealize her marriage, although the Prince of Wales's craving for constant distraction made it impossible for him to live at home with

---

* Eddy was now nineteen.

his family for more than a very short time. She even went so far as to entertain his mistresses. The professional beauty Lillie Langtry, who was the Prince of Wales's first "official" mistress, recalled how Alexandra cared for her after she became ill during a dinner party at Marlborough House:

> The Princess, so kind and compassionate always, immediately told me to hurry home to bed, which I thankfully did. Half a hour later the Household Physician, Francis Laking, was ushered into my room, having been sent by command of the Princess of Wales to see me and report to her on my condition. By the next afternoon I was feeling better, and was lying on the sofa about tea-time, when the butler suddenly announced Her Royal Highness. The honour of the unexpected visit brought me at once to my feet ill though I felt, but the Princess insisted on my lying down again, whilst she herself made tea, chatting kindly and graciously. She always used a specially manufactured violet scent, and I recall exclaiming on the delicious perfume and her solicitous answer that she feared possibly it was too strong for me.

Just as she continued to regard her sons as innocent babes, even after they had grown well into manhood, Alexandra seemed to prefer everyone in a childlike mold. For Princess Louise's nineteenth birthday, she gave her a children's party and she caused great embarrassment to one of her nieces, a lady in her twenties, by sending her presents suitable for a child of ten.

Alexandra's whole existence was politely removed from reality. Consequently, it did not seem unnatural to her when her husband announced that he was taking Eddy with him on a trip to Egypt and India scheduled to begin in October 1889. Eddy had been away in Dublin with his regiment, the 10th Hussars, at least that is what Alexandra had been told, and she had no reason to doubt it. She had not seen her son for almost a year.

Sir Edward Bradford, V.C., who was later to become Commissioner of the Metropolitan Police, was assigned to guard Eddy at all times. The tour of southern India had been prescribed with the one intention of hiding Eddy from the public eye. There was polo in the morning and in the evening. In Bombay, Eddy was

met by streets lined with troops and crowds hailing his arrival. At
Ganesh Khird, after a full dress dinner, he received the nation's
princes and finally the Rajah of Kolapore. Eddy sat in their midst,
his face pale and drawn, his neck covered with garlands of orchids.

Dr. Gull had felt that Eddy's condition was improved, although
the daily requirement of iodide of potassium was continued. As
long as he was watched, and never allowed to venture anywhere
on his own, he could attend state dinners, greet foreign royalty,
and superficially appear as if he were as free as any royal prince
was allowed to be. According to plan, his father had accompanied
him to Egypt aboard H.M.S. *Osborne*. Perfunctorily, they had
both attended the wedding in Athens of Constantine, Duke of
Sparta, heir to the Greek throne, with Princess Sophie of Prussia,
one of Kaiser Wilhelm's sisters. Then on October 31, Eddy's father had taken leave of him in Port Said, placing him in Edward
Bradford's custody.

When he reached Hyderabad, Eddy was met by His Highness
the Nizam, accompanied by his private secretary and aide-de-
camp, Nawab Asfar Jung, who was colorfully presented as "one of
the best riders, pig-stickers, and tent-peggers" in India. The
Nizam took him deer hunting using a hooded hunting leopard.
Eddy watched as the leopard, once unhooded, tore down a deep
ravine and was soon among the deer, which fled before him. The
leopard had chosen his quarry well, however, and when Eddy and
the Nizam rode up on their horses, the leopard was sucking blood
from his victim's throat. The leopard, when hooded by his keeper,
immediately let go of his prey and was taken back to his cart,
where he was given a bowl of antelope's blood as a reward for obe-
dience and good behavior.

That evening the Nizam gave a banquet in Eddy's honor. Big
bulging buns were served and the guests were admonished not to
pass them up. With a prick of a fork, it was shown that the buns
were not solid, *and that there was something alive inside*. As each
of the buns was opened, a waxbill fluttered out of its pastry tomb
and flew about the room, chirping merrily and rejoicing at its own
recovered liberty. Several pies were cut open, and, greatly exceed-
ing the number of those recounted in the nursery rhyme, no less

than six dozen birds were released and began to fly and sing. After dinner was served on ice-plates made of sugar, the Nizam stood up:

"I rise to propose the health of His Royal Highness, Prince Albert Victor of Wales, who has been graciously pleased to honour me tonight. Although His Royal Highness's visit is a private one, we Indians cannot for a moment forget that, after his royal father, he stands nearest to the throne of Great Britain, and of that Greater Britain which includes India. In this splendid empire, over which the sun never sets, he will be welcomed wherever he goes, but nowhere will be welcomed more loyally than he is here in Hyderabad, both by myself and my people. I beg His Royal Highness to accept for himself, and convey to Her Majesty, the Queen Empress, assurances of my devoted friendship and loyalty, and the devotion and loyalty of my subjects. I will now call upon you to drink to the health of His Royal Highness, Prince Albert Victor of Wales, with the prayer that God may grant him long life and a brilliant and glorious career."

There is no record of Eddy's reply. It is assumed that he probably proposed the health of the Nizam and thanked him for his loyalty to the Queen.

Leaving Hyderabad, Eddy's party traveled by train over the river Krishna into Madras through groves of tamarind trees and fields of wheat, maize, and rice. The ground was covered with cassia and date palms and it was said that one could pick up with his fingers great congealed drops of medicine gum.

Before the Government House in Madras, Eddy was called upon to deliver a speech. It was brief and well thought out:

"I beg to thank you most heartily for the cordial and pleasant terms in which you bid me welcome to this capital of the Madras Presidency. Ever since I landed in India I have been greeted by its people with an enthusiastic kindness and good will to which I know I have no personal claim. But I can assure you that it is all the greater delight to me, when I realize that in the reception given to myself, your loyalty and devotion to Her Majesty, the Queen Empress are made so unmistakably clear."

There were more banquets and hunting parties before Eddy moved on to Mysore, the Keddahs, and Travancore. Meanwhile, the Indian press noted that it was "Her Majesty's Orders" that Eddy's visit should be private. It was also recognized by at least one or two journalists that Edward Bradford was taking infinite pains to carry this order out: accompanying the Prince wherever he went and not allowing him to be interviewed by reporters. All public utterances, such as the speech in front of the Government House in Madras, were kept short, to the point, and extremely patronizing. It had been difficult for the Indian authorities to accept this restricted sense of "privacy," and they could not help but urge that the Prince should see the people as they were, that he should visit the outlying villages and learn for himself what a Hindu hamlet and a Hindu peasant were really like. Eddy was described in their newspapers as having "so strong a resemblance to his charming mother† as to be already familiar to the people." Ladies wrote odes to him and his visit was celebrated in verse in almost every language spoken in the country. He took in all the tourist sights in one-hundred-and-seventeen-degree heat, including the prison in which Tippoo Sahib had imprisoned the British soldiers (the Black Hole of Calcutta), the memorial at Cawnpore, Akbar's Fort, the Taj Mahal, and the Moti Musjid, and, according to one member of his party, Captain Holford, proved himself to be an expert at killing:

> After a mile and a half of tracking we came upon the bull in some thick jungle. I saw him thirty yards off before H.R.H. did, and covered him with my rifle. H.R.H. fired, and the bull fell. He fired again . . . the bull plunged on his head toward us. I put a .500 bullet into his head, and the Prince fired six more shots into him, until he was quite dead.

Eddy visited the Leper Hospital in Jungagad where the unfortunate inmates sang the national anthem, and, according to the press, "seemed much gratified by his visit." Then in mid-December, the Prince and his party sailed upon the ship *Kristra* for Rangoon. But the stifling heat of the Bay of Bengal erupted into a monsoon, as Captain Holford complained bitterly about "the French cook on board, who will send up nothing but the richest of made dishes."

† Alexandra had visited India with her husband in 1879.

On Christmas Day, Eddy attended services at the Palace of King Theebaw where, as Captain Holford noted, "the communion table covers the king's throne, which is surmounted by a pinnacle, and is called the centre of the universe."

Traveling to Kanchrapara after the first of January, Eddy continued to hunt and be feasted in village after village, described in rhapsodic words by an accompanying journalist:

> . . . the dark Indian night, the long lines of soft lights rising tier upon tier against the dark background of the trees, the swarthy conjurers with their weird deceits, the barbaric music, the rhythmical swaying of the Nautch girls, the tempestuous frenzy of the kuttak dance—and in the midst of it our soldier and sailor Prince . . .

Meanwhile, six thousand miles away, the London press noted that there had been no Ripper murders for over a year. Melville Macnaghten, a Scotland Yard detective who was later to head the C.I.D., had formulated in writing the theory that was soon to be accepted by all but the most discerning, that "the murderer's brain gave way altogether after his awful glut in Miller's Court, and that he immediately committed suicide." Such a conclusion perhaps did not help Albert Backert of the Whitechapel Vigilance Committee rest any easier, and it certainly could not have overcome the terrible anxiety of a prominent West End physician who, while Eddy was being feted and praised in Calcutta, suffered a major stroke in his home just off Grosvenor Square at 74 Brook Street.

But it did quiet the fears of most Londoners who were intent on seeing the murders end, even if the killer's identity was never revealed. The myth of Jack the Ripper might become a never-to-be-solved mystery, but the political life of England could continue under the leadership of Lord Salisbury and his Conservative government. The Prince of Wales would soon be off to attend the Kaiser's birthday party on January 27. He would be armed with a list of possible princesses, compiled by Queen Victoria, for Eddy to marry. The first name on the list was the Kaiser's youngest sister, Princess Margaret, who was nicknamed "Mossy."

Chapter 15

HÉLÈNE

It was always Sir William Gull's belief that Eddy's moral derangement was physical in origin. His treatment of Eddy's dementia was limited to attempting to ameliorate his syphilitic condition, although he continued using hypnotic suggestion until he was certain that Eddy was cured. The symptoms of syphilis might reappear, but the violent delusions had ceased.

Eddy would not be the first member of the Royal Family to suffer from mental illness, but the ordeal of completely hiding him from the eyes of the public was insurmountable. The trip to India would be followed by more treatment until it was proved that he was able to live what could pass for a normal life.

He had never been normal. Not even as a child. And this area troubled Dr. Gull. Yet his years as a physician had taught him to treat only the physical disorder, never the patient.

It had been almost half a century since Gull had gained the gold medal at London University for the examination he almost had not written. Shortly thereafter he coined the phrase for himself that was to guide his work and his life: *Fools and savages ex-*

plain; wise men investigate. It was a theorem that had been tested many times, but he had never given in to assuming that he had a knowledge which he, in fact, did not possess, nor had he ever consciously allowed himself to form a conclusion without evidence.

Perhaps if he had never met the nephew of the treasurer of Guy's Hospital, he might not have become a doctor. Instead, he might have gone to sea and become a sailor. That was an area of his nature that he had never really looked into.

On that afternoon in January, when Dr. Gull's lifeless body was discovered in the study of his home, a sheet of paper was found on his desk. It was not only about Eddy; it was the conclusion of everything that he had struggled to observe:

> The so-called disintegration of moral nature, and its re-establishment by reciprocal control of the nerve-centres, is a proper work of science. But here we reach a region in which our anatomical conceptions are sure to be at fault, since they reach but to form and not to composition.
>
> The solution of the mystery seems so near, and yet so far off. We have evidence from the history of the earth that incalculable time and incalculable circumstances have been the problem. All the forces of our planet are in the problem. And not only the forces of the earth in matter and gravitation, but also the celestial forces of light and heat, both primal and present. And further, the eocene germ forces their constant operation and augmental through all time; and further, our need of education into the study of nature, and the works and workings for a successful inquiry, are all considerations which show how far off we are from knowing what we are, and how we come to be.
>
> Doubtless for the ends of practice we have knowledge enough at least for our moral guidance, and science continually though gradually adds to our consciousness of life; but for full knowledge we are *infants in the dark.*

On June 23, His Royal Highness, Prince Albert Victor Christian Edward was created Duke of Clarence and Avondale. Sponsored by his father, he took his seat in the House of Lords. How enigmatic it must have seemed to Lord Salisbury to gaze across those revered chambers at the personage who almost toppled his government, to accept as his peer the ermine and red velvet robed figure of Jack the Ripper.

His only consolation was that the title *Clarence* had proved ill-fated in three out of four cases. The first Duke of Clarence, third son of Edward III, had died without an heir. The second Clarence had perished in battle fighting for his elder brother, Henry V. Edward IV's younger brother became the third Duke of Clarence in 1461 but was soon after tried before Parliament for slandering the Crown and organizing a rebellion in the north of England. He was secretly put to death in the Tower of London on February 18, 1478, although later the rumor was circulated that he had been drowned in a barrel of malmsey wine. On four occasions—the fourth was William IV—the title had become extinct upon the death of its bearer, and Salisbury must certainly have desired that once more history might repeat itself.

From all appearances, Eddy was not long for this world. He had returned from India looking desperately ill. In the meantime, every attempt at securing for him a proper wife had failed. His attractive cousin "Alicky," Princess of Hesse, daughter of Princess Alice, had turned him down. And he had rejected "Mossy" (Princess Margaret of Prussia), after Queen Victoria had finally admitted that she was "not regularly pretty." Instead, he announced his love for Princess Hélène, the daughter of the Comte de Paris, a pretender to the French throne.

Following the death of the Comte de Chambord in 1883, the Comte de Paris had been welcomed by the extremely powerful Royalist Party as France's rightful King. He had sued for, and obtained, the royal châteaux which had been nationalized by the Republic, but following the marriage of his daughter Marie Amélie to Dom Carlos, Duque de Braganza, and heir to the Portuguese throne, the Republicans expelled the Comte de Paris and his family and confiscated their property. Arriving at Dover, the Comte had declared his belief that monarchy was the ideal form of French government and he had been joined in this sentiment by Eddy's father, the Prince of Wales, whose great affection for the French and his wish for an *entente cordiale*, immediately antagonized his nephew, Kaiser Wilhelm.

The Comte de Paris' daughter Hélène was a beautiful, innocent young creature and there is no doubt that she was strongly attracted to Eddy. But it was destined to be a disastrous choice. She was Roman Catholic.

Princess Alexandra was aware of the obstacles. Under the British Constitution, the heir to the throne was forbidden to marry a Roman Catholic. But Eddy cleverly had mentioned his choice only to her, and Alexandra, believing her son to be brokenhearted by the Hessian Princess Alicky's refusal, in addition to being blinded by her own hatred of Kaiser Wilhelm, foolishly conspired to help him. She invited the French Princess to Mar Lodge, her daughter Princess Louise's Scottish home. There in August 1890, Eddy and Hélène became engaged.

Alexandra was determined that the couple should marry, but her major obstacle was overcoming the Queen's disapproval. Hearing about her grandson's romance, Victoria had already written a strong warning letter. Alexandra, ignoring her mother-in-law's wishes, urged Eddy and Hélène to make a surprise visit to Balmoral and appeal to the Queen in person.

It was something that Eddy was reluctant to do, but Alexandra was so persuasive that at last the journey was arranged. Eddy and Hélène traveled by coach to Balmoral where, taken by storm, Victoria could not resist their entreaties. She was so overcome by the sight of *young love* that she gave the couple her blessing.

Princess Hélène would change her religion if necessary and become a Protestant, and Victoria, who was both touched and agitated, promised to do what she could to help them.

Victoria's minister in attendance, A. J. Balfour, wrote immediately to his uncle, Lord Salisbury:

> Will it be believed that neither the Queen nor the young Prince, nor Princess Hélène see anything which is not romantic, interesting, touching and praiseworthy in the young lady giving up a religion, to which *she still professes devoted attachment,* in order to marry the man on whom she says she has set her heart! . . . At the best it is the sacrifice of religion for love, while at the worst it is the sacrifice of religion for a throne . . .

Hélène's mother, the Comtesse de Paris, was a masculine woman. After shooting or deerstalking, she was fond of smoking the Prince of Wales's best cigars. Her reaction was immediate. Her daughter could leave the Church of Rome and enter the Church of England following the marriage. But her husband, the Comte, rigidly opposed the idea. His daughter must never become a Protestant. To this end, he was supported by an unexpected source: Lord Salisbury. Salisbury was coldly caustic to the efforts of Princess Alexandra in trying to bring about the marriage. He reacted by using every means at his disposal as Prime Minister and by composing detailed memoranda upon the dangerous legal and political aspects of the affair. When the Prince of Wales, primed by his wife, casually asked Salisbury if it would be possible for Hélène to retain her Roman Catholicism, though her children were brought up in the Church of England, the Prime Minister retorted that he should quickly abandon the idea. Salisbury warned him that the anger of the middle and lower classes would endanger the throne if anyone even guessed that the Royal Family contemplated such an act. Frustrated and disturbed, the Prince of Wales wrote to his son Prince George on October 12:

> What the ultimate result may be, God only knows . . . I am not very sanguine.

Meanwhile, Salisbury laughed out loud when Alexandra argued that "apostasy ought to be accepted as conclusive proof of Hélène's disinterested love." But finally it was Hélène herself who set out to break the deadlock. She went personally to the Pope.

Pope Leo XIII was a diplomat who had long urged a revival of the philosophy of St. Thomas Aquinas. He especially supported Aquinas' doctrine of a world ruled by purpose, where the right and the good coincide, and where all men ought to act well because that was the way to be happy. In addition, it served his political purposes.

When the British Government withdrew their diplomatic envoys from the Papal consuls in Malta and Gibraltar in 1884, because the Pope was no longer ruler of a sovereign independent state, Leo XIII planned to revenge the heretics' affront to the Vicar of Christ. Hélène's visit to the Vatican became his opportunity.

Hélène had gone to the Pope for reassurance and to implore him to solve the crisis created by her father's opposition to her marriage. The Pope scolded the terrified young Princess, threatening her with eternal hell-fire should she depart from the One True Faith in order to wed the heretic Eddy. Having performed his duty, the sanctimonious "servant of the servants of God" gave her his Papal Benediction and sent her away stricken and inconsolable.

After Alexandra had guided the matter past both her husband and the Queen, Salisbury's scorn, in addition to the Comte de Paris' opposition and the vindictive affront of Leo XIII, left her disillusioned and bitter. "All we can do now is to wait and see what time can do for us and trust in God to help us," she wrote to Prince George; "in the meantime they go on corresponding and loving one another from a distance."

Alexandra's sad conclusion was not exactly true. That autumn, Eddy had, in fact, returned to the company of his old friends, the homosexuals who frequented such queer establishments as The Crown in Charing Cross Road, The Pakenham in Knightsbridge Green, and that extremely ostentatious gathering place known as The Hundred Guineas Club. There, clad in ballgowns and hoop dresses, members assumed female names; Eddy was called "Victoria."

By the first of the year, his dissipations were commonly known throughout London. And, then, finally, the inevitable incident occurred which was to seal his doom once and for all.

Chapter 16

THE FINAL MURDER

At 7 P.M., on the evening of February 11, 1891, Ship's Fireman James Saddler was given his pay and discharged from the S.S. *Fez*, lying in St. Katharine's Docks. He headed for The Princess Alice pub, off Whitechapel Road, where he hoped to meet Frances Coles, a prostitute whom he had spent the night with at a lodging house in Thrawl Street eighteen months before.

Frances was waiting for him but insisted they go elsewhere because the customers at The Princess Alice, whenever they saw her with someone with money, expected her to join them for drinks. Together, they left and set out on an evening of carousing at other pubs in the area. After several hours, Saddler bought half a pint of whisky to take home and he and Frances finished the night in an eightpenny lodging on Dorset Street. They did not get up until noon the following day.

As soon as they hit the street, they continued drinking. They first visited The Bell in Middlesex Street, where they stayed for two hours. Saddler now promised to buy Frances a new hat, and, as they headed for a milliner's shop in Baker's Row, gave her half a crown. He then waited outside.

When Frances appeared in a short while with the news that some elastic had to be stitched on before the hat was ready, they adjourned to a nearby pub to wait. Returning to the milliner's shop, Frances picked up her new hat. Saddler insisted that she throw her old one away, but she refused, pinning it to her dress.

By now, Saddler was feeling pretty drunk, but Frances prodded him to stop for more whiskies at The Marlborough Head in Brick Lane. After several hours, they left there, both of them staggering down Thrawl Street. It was then that Saddler was hit on the head and knocked to the ground by a woman in a crimson shawl. As he tried to get up, he was surrounded by several men who began kicking him. They then robbed him of his watch and all his money before escaping down the street.

Saddler, now penniless, was forced to go back to St. Katharine's Docks to get more money. There, he once again ran into difficulty. The shipping office was closed and he ended up swearing and taking out his anger on the men on the dock gates. Though there was a police constable nearby, one of the dockers finally cornered him and beat him up.

Recovering after a few hours, Saddler managed to hobble back to the lodging house on Dorset Street where he had spent the night before with Frances Coles. He found her in the kitchen with her head on her arms. She was drunk and out of money. Saddler tried to persuade the manager of the establishment to let him have a bed, insisting that he had four pounds and fifteen shillings ship's pay coming to him. But he was promptly evicted, although Frances was permitted to stay the night.

Saddler, at this point, was in a terrible state. His only recourse was to set off for London Hospital to have his injuries cared for. He was stopped at once by a policeman, who observed the blood on his face and clothes. Saddler admitted to him that he had been in two fights and had been cut with a knife or a bottle. Hearing the word "knife," the constable immediately searched him, over Saddler's protestations that he never carried one. The policeman finally helped him to the hospital, where Saddler's head was bandaged. He was permitted to spend the night on a couch in the Accident Ward.

The following morning, February 13, Saddler hastened to the shipping office and picked up his four pounds and fifteen shillings. He then paid for a bed and spent the rest of the day drinking by himself. That night he slept alone.

At 11 P.M., on the evening of February 13, while James Saddler was moodily drinking and trying to recover from his injuries, Police Constable Thompson of H Division discovered, under the railway arch between Royal Mint Street and Chamber Street, a woman with her throat cut and her lower body mutilated. She was still alive when he found her, and it was apparent that the constable had barely missed confronting the killer, who obviously escaped when he spotted the glow of the approaching policeman's bull's-eye lantern. However, lying in the gutter beside the body was an important clue: a woman's brand-new hat. In addition, *an older-looking hat was still pinned to the front of her dress.*

Frances Coles's "friend" was described by the manager of the milliner's shop in Baker's Row. This description was corroborated by the proprietor of the lodging house in Dorset Street who recalled that the man had been bleeding and had tried to secure a room for both himself and the murder victim on the night of February 12. A trail led to London Hospital, where the suspect had been treated at the Out-Patient's Department. The treating doctor remembered that his clothing had been saturated with blood.

James Saddler was arrested for the murder of Frances Coles, and was the immediate focus of an upheaval which spread to the House of Commons. The press and public had waited two years for this moment. As rumors gathered, it soon became evident to all but the most discerning that the police had finally captured Jack the Ripper.

In Parliament on February 17, Home Secretary Matthews, who was well aware of the Ripper's true identity, was confronted by Mr. H. J. Wilson of Holmfirth, York.

> WILSON: I beg to ask the Home Secretary whether it is true, as stated by the man Saddler, who is charged in connection with the Whitechapel murder, in the course of his cross-ex-

amination, that he was not in good trim to cross-examine as he was cold and hungry, that he repeated the statement over and over again; and whether it is the custom to bring prisoners to the public-courts who have had nothing to eat?

MATTHEWS: No, Sir. It is not true. The Commissioner of Police informs me that Saddler had his regular meals on Sunday, and his breakfast on Monday. *His dinner on Monday was being prepared for him when he was summoned to the Court.** He had it afterwards.

WILSON: Then how is it that Superintendent Arnold, when the man complained, said to him, "You shall have something."

MATTHEWS: I really cannot answer as to Superintendent Arnold's motives.

In the Parliamentary session on February 26, a strange focus was put upon Saddler's drinking, which gradually revealed a much greater feeling of unrest over his indictment and the Government's flagrant attempt to railroad a conviction. Mr. Esslemont, of Aberdeen, questioned Matthews.

ESSLEMONT: I beg to ask the Secretary of State for the Home Department whether his attention has been called to the evidence of the police before the Coroner of East London at the inquiry regarding the death of Frances Coles on Friday last, from which it appears that the man Saddler was left outside the dock gates in a state of intoxication, such as to be thought unable to go on board his ship; that he was struck down and severely bruised in presence of or without remonstrance on the part of the police; and whether, if the man was drunk as described, he was entitled to protection; or, if not, to be taken into custody by the police?

MATTHEWS: The Commissioner of Police informs me that he has only seen a newspaper account of the evidence, and there is nothing in that to bear out the allegation that Saddler was struck down and severely bruised in the presence of the police. The only constable who saw him at the dock gate considered that, although he had been drinking, he was not in such a state of intoxication as to warrant his being taken into custody.

---

* Which was the obvious answer to Mr. Wilson's question: Saddler had not eaten and was most probably hungry.

ESSLEMONT: Has the attention of the right honorable Gentleman been called to the fact that *in the sworn evidence* it is stated that this policeman was asked to turn away, and that he did go away 30 yards?

Matthews was caught by surprise, but quickly responded.

MATTHEWS: No, Sir; I have not had a Report of such evidence, but I will make inquiry.

Although Matthews was jockeying for position until Saddler's trial progressed to the hoped-for conclusion, the question of the seaman's drinking and the irresponsibility of the police cropped up in another form, on March 9, raised by a second Member of Parliament, Mr. J. Rowntree of Scarborough. The astounding point was that so much time and discussion was taken up in Great Britain's House of Commons over an accused man's drinking habits, rather than if, in fact, he were receiving a fair trial.

ROWNTREE: I beg to ask the Secretary of State for the Home Department if his attention has been drawn to the continual and excessive drinking at public houses disclosed by the evidence in the inquest on the late Whitechapel murder, in which Saddler was described by two witnesses as "very drunk and the deceased woman was stated to be half dazed with drink"; if it is correct that 2,309 persons were apprehended during the year 1889 for drunkenness in the Whitechapel Police District; how many of the holders of licenses in that district were proceeded against for permitting drunkenness during that year, and with what results; and if he will consider whether steps can be taken either to make the law or the administration of the law in the Metropolis, more efficient in checking drunkenness?

Home Secretary Matthews responded by being as vague as possible, never answering the question, but defending everyone involved.

MATTHEWS: Yes, Sir; I gather from statements made before the Coroner that the man Saddler had been drinking from house to house. The figures quoted in the second paragraph are correct. There was one case where proceedings were taken for permitting drunkenness, and this was dismissed by the Magistrate. The Commissioner of Police assures me that every effort is made for the efficient enforcement of the law, and the figures quoted show that the police are not inactive. But the honorable Member is doubtless aware that there are great difficulties if proof in cases where publicans are charged with permitting drunkenness, and I do not think those difficulties will be removed by alteration of the law.

Once again, on March 9, Mr. Esslemont, of Aberdeen, prodded Home Secretary Matthews for the information he had asked for on February 26.

ESSLEMONT: I beg to ask the Secretary of State for the Home Department if he has yet received a Report from the Chief Commissioner in regard to the evidence of the police as affecting their conduct in the case of Saddler.

Home Secretary Matthews, obviously straining to avoid the challenge, replied that all evidence was contained in the Coroner's depositions. M.P. Esslemont, however, did not let up.

ESSLEMONT: Can access be obtained to the official evidence?
MATTHEWS: No, Sir; the Coroner's depositions are only made public in the event of a verdict of murder or manslaughter on the occasion of the trial by the authorities.

This meant that no records would be released until *an actual verdict* was reached. In addition to this, the indigent Saddler *had been denied all legal aid.*

But Saddler continued to protest his innocence. In desperation, he wrote to the Secretary of the Stokers' Union, begging him to engage a solicitor in his behalf. Finally, barrister Harry Wilson was hired by the Union to defend him.

Despite the efforts of the Government and the police to prove Saddler's guilt, barrister Wilson won out. He was able to show that in every previous Ripper murder, Saddler had been at sea.

At last the Government and the police were forced to abandon their case. Saddler was released and the murder of Frances Coles was classified as unsolved.

It was an incident that had shaken Lord Salisbury to the core.

There was no further question in his mind that Eddy's identity could be hidden. With a ruthlessness that he had never before exercised, Salisbury moved to end the whole nasty business once and for all.

Chapter 17

THE PRISONER

George Selwyn, one of London's most notorious profligates, on March 28, 1757, had attended the ghastly execution of Damiens, who had made an attempt on the life of Louis XV. Damiens had stabbed the King as he was entering his carriage at Versailles and, in consequence, was sentenced to be torn in pieces by horses in the Place de Grève. Selwyn, who loved to attend executions, often disguising himself in female dress, traveled to Paris for the express purpose of witnessing the last excruciating moments of the would-be assassin. Mingling with the crowd, Selwyn approached too near to the scaffold. He was suddenly seized by one of the executioners and had to explain that he had made the journey from London solely with a view to be present at the punishment and death of Damiens. The executioner responded by positioning Selwyn in the front row, announcing to the crowd, "Make way for this man; *C'est un Anglais, et un amateur.*"

The archetype of the sadistic Englishman was further patented by the poet Swinburne, who was so strongly attracted to the writings of the Marquis de Sade that he literally paraphrased them in his play *Atlanta in Calydon:*

> Nature averse to crime? I tell you, nature lives and breathes by it; hungers at all her pores for bloodshed, aches in all her nerves for the help of sin, yearns with all her heart for the furtherance of cruelty. Nature forbid that thing or this? Nay, the best or worst of you will never go so far as she would have you; no criminal will come up to the measure of her crimes, no destruction seems to her destructive enough. We, when we do evil, can disorganize a little matter, shed a little blood, quench a little breath at the door of a perishable body; this we can do, and call it a crime. Unnatural is it? Good friend, it is by criminal things and deeds unnatural that nature works and moves and has her being . . . Friends, if we would be one with nature, let us continually do evil with all our might. But what evil is here for us to do, when the whole body of things is evil? The day's spider kills the day's fly and calls it a crime? . . . And what are the worst sins we can do—we who live for a day and die in a night? a few murders . . .

Eddy's lover, James Stephen, was the primeval embodiment of a whole sadistic tradition. He once had written bitterly about a girl he had known:

> *I did not like her: and I should not mind*
> *If she were done away with, killed or ploughed.*

And concerning a stranger whose indifference and lack of caring "didst rouse me from my slumbers mad with pain," James wished:

> *Oh may'st thou suffer tortures without end:*
> *May friends with glowing pincers rend thy brain,*
> *And beetles batten on thy blackened face!*

How much more, however, he gave the world by creating the literary character "Jack the Ripper!" It was a name that would forever chill the heart, even though its bearer was no more than the pathetic embodiment of a hopelessly deranged psyche.

On November 21, 1891, James Stephen was committed, by the powers who ruled England, to the lunatic ward of St. Andrew's Hospital, Northampton.

The decision regarding Eddy had to be more complexly formulated. The Prince of Wales suggested that his son be sent on a tour of the more remote colonies, principally Australia and Canada. But at this point, not knowing the true situation, Queen Victoria expressed her desire that Eddy should visit the major cities of Europe. Bertie was forced to reply:

> It is difficult to explain to you the reasons we do not consider it desirable for him to make lengthened stays in foreign capitals.

Whether the final decision was made exclusively by Salisbury, by the Prince of Wales, or by both of them at once, Eddy's fate was at last sealed. Despite Victoria's continuing attempts at choosing for him a suitable spouse (culminating in Eddy's official engagement to May Teck:* their wedding was scheduled for February 27, 1892), there was no way that Eddy would ever succeed to the throne of England.

As the last cycle of Eddy's life was pushed toward its finality, it is reasonable to imagine that certain means were introduced to bring it to a swift conclusion. In place of the regular administrations of iodide of potassium, Eddy most probably was given daily injections of morphine. It effected relief from his pain and produced deep sleep. In addition, it created a sense of euphoria.

Finally, when he was confined to a rest home in Ascot, the dosages were steadily increased until the sleep condition became permanent.

Historically, Eddy died at Sandringham on January 14, 1892, after a sudden attack of influenza.†

---

* In 1886, Sir Henry Ponsonby had noted: "Princess May seems out of the question as the Prince and Princess of Wales have no love for the parents and the boy does not care for the girl." Alexandra gradually encouraged the union, however, prompted by the fact that the Teck family were her Danish cousins. Shortly before the engagement was announced, Ponsonby observed that it would be a marriage of convenience, yet could not resist attributing heroic motives to the Princess: "I am told he [Eddy] does not care for Princess May of Teck and she appears to be too proud to take the trouble of running after him for which I rather admire her." Most probably, however, on some deeper level, although they hardly knew each other, Princess May sensed that her betrothed possessed a complex, deeply troubled, and perhaps threatening nature.
† In the late 1890s, Dr. Thomas Stowell met the head gardener, W. Watters, who had been at Sandringham on the date of Eddy's death. When Stowell made some casual remark about Eddy's dying there, the gardener replied in surprise, "Did he!" Then added, "Not while I was there."

A service confined to members of the household was held at the Sandringham Church, but *the body was not revealed.*

The actual burial took place at Windsor, a short distance from the rest home in Ascot. Even though Alexandra had insisted that her son be buried at Sandringham with the other members of the family, the Prince of Wales would not permit it. No risk must be taken that Prince George's life might be overshadowed by the despicable image of his brother.

Alexandra's attendance at the funeral was forbidden, but the poor woman finally persuaded her husband to allow her to watch from the gallery known as "the Queen's closet." She confined to her daughters: "I shall hide upon the staircase, in a corner, unknown to the world."

The Prince of Wales wore his uniform. The pallbearers were officers of the 10th Hussars. Foreign royalty circled the body like figures in a waxworks: the Grand Duke Alexis, to represent the Czar of Russia, the Crown Prince of Denmark, Prince Frederick Leopold of Prussia, representing the Kaiser, Prince Philip of Saxe-Coburg and Gotha for the King of the Belgians, the Duke of Oporto for the King of Portugal, Duke Albert of Würtenberg for the King of Würtenberg, Baron Steuber for the Grand Duke of Mecklenburg, Chamberlain Von Klench for the Duke of Cumberland, Baron Westwiller for the Grand Duke of Hesse . . .

There was no sunlight. It was a bleak wintry day. Beneath the banners of the knights and the golden altar cloth, the coffin was inscribed:

HIS ROYAL HIGHNESS ALBERT VICTOR CHRISTIAN EDWARD, DUKE OF CLARENCE AND AVONDALE K.G., K.P., MAJOR 10TH ROYAL HUSSARS: BORN 8TH JANUARY 1864 AT FROGMORE, WINDSOR; DIED 14TH JANUARY 1892 AT SANDRINGHAM, NORFOLK.

In an ornate golden tomb erected in the Albert Memorial Chapel, Eddy was buried alone and apart from the rest of his family. Present was one loving gesture: a hanging wreath of *immortelles* inscribed simply: *Hélène.*

Following the funeral, the French Princess had a conversation with Queen Victoria. *"Je l'aimais tant,"* she remarked. Then she added, with a tear in her eyes, *"Il était si bon."*

Exactly twenty days after Eddy's death, James Kenneth Stephen died. His fate had been much grimmer than Eddy's. He had been starved to death in the lunatic asylum of St. Andrew's Hospital, Northampton.

Within a few days, a final precaution was taken: every shred of communication between Eddy and James was destroyed.

The normal practice of Scotland Yard was that once a criminal case was closed, it was marked closed for a hundred years. The reason for this is that it was thought that any shorter period would not guarantee the anonymity of the highly confidential statements made to the police during the course of an investigation. The hundred-year ruling safely covered one man's lifetime.

Shortly after the deaths of Eddy and his lover, James Stephen, in 1892, the official Jack the Ripper File was sealed by the Metropolitan Police and Home Secretary Matthews' office, and designated to be hidden away for the legal hundred-year period. The file's cover was marked with the profoundest vertification of the murderer's identity: CLOSED UNTIL 1992.

Chapter 18

THE FILE

I have seen the Jack the Ripper File. Through a friend in the Metropolitan Police, I was able to gain access to MEPOL 3/140-2 and HOME OFFICE FILE 144/220/A49301 located in the Public Records Office in London. I was not surprised to find that the contents have been gutted.

In the Home Office File, alone, most of the first 227 folders are either missing or destroyed. When I asked about this, I was not given an explanation.

The Metropolitan Police File (MEPOL 3/140-2) contains three packets of loose sheets of paper in brown-wrapped folders bound with white string. On the top of each folder is stamped "1992," the date when the file can be opened to the general public. I noted that each folder had been officially closed in 1892.

Two of the brown-wrapped packets contain letters from London citizens offering suggestions on how the murderer might be captured. Most of these are amusing, such as the one that suggested that the killer's hiding place was an old vault in the Jews' Cemetery. The same letter also posed the possibility that when the Ripper escaped, he most probably traveled through the underground sewers, at the same time tearing into shreds his bloodstained coat and scattering its pieces underground. The writer had obviously never been in an underground sewer.

Another letter which I could not completely laugh at pictured the killer as an "upper or wealthy sort," one of those who might kill for pleasure, "without regard to any law but his own will." And of course there were the usual crank letters, pinning the murders on someone's cousin or nephew or on a mysterious stranger just moved into the new house down the road. An obvious suspect was the watchman in Mitre Square. One lady dreamed that she had seen him peeping out of the warehouse door and laughing at the policemen as they rounded the corner. But the most revealing statements were made by several ladies who wished to sacrifice themselves to catch the murderer. They would take the place of the prostitutes in Whitechapel, even though it meant that they might be murdered in the process.

The third packet in the Metropolitan Police File is the most disturbing of all. It contains several slim brown folders, each with a victim's name across the top. The folders, themselves, contain nothing but published newspaper accounts of the murders. There is not even a coroner's report present, excepting the highly misleading one written by Dr. Bond which states that the murderer was "probably middle-aged . . . without regular occupation, but with some small income or pension."

What is left of the Home Office Files have been rifled as well. The only investigative report they contain is the handwritten memorandum of Inspector Abberline detailing his plan to use George Hutchinson, who had seen Marie Jeanette Kelly's killer on the morning she was murdered.

Obviously whoever gutted the Home Office Files regarded Abberline's report as of little importance. But when one considers that Hutchinson's description of the killer (about five feet eight inches tall, with a pale complexion, dark hair, and a slight moustache curled up at each end) perfectly fitted Eddy, and that Hutchinson was not allowed to testify at the abortive inquest held at Shoreditch on November 12, it becomes an extremely significant document.

With this in mind, I made a special request that a copy be made of the document.

At 9 P.M. on the evening of the day I perused the file, I received an unusual telephone call at my hotel from the Office of the Home Secretary. They wanted to know exactly why I wanted to see the file. I carefully explained that I was doing a book on mass murderers, and in no way intended to write more than a few pages on the most famous mass murderer of all. This explanation seemed to satisfy them, but I felt a slight trace of anxiety when they asked why I wished to copy a document from their file.

I explained that since I was not allowed to make notes of the file's contents (I was not even permitted a pencil and paper), that I needed the actual wording of the document in order to be certain that whatever I might quote from it was correct. After a few moments' pause, I was told that I could have a copy of the document. It would be sent to me.

The following day I paid for the document to be reproduced. But, as I anticipated, I never received it.

Suspecting that once the Home Secretary's Office was fully alerted to my methods of obtaining information, that they might attempt to thwart me in some way, on the day that I had studied the file, during the lunch hour period, I had approached a young man left alone on duty at the Photostat machine and slipped him a few pound notes to make a quick copy of the document for me. I explained that I was leaving by plane that night for New York. Although he related that it was against the normal procedure, he quietly photostated the document. Perhaps before the file is officially opened to the public, this document too will disappear with all the others. In consideration of that possibility, it is reproduced below in its entirety:

METROPOLITAN POLICE

CENTRAL OFFICER'S

SPECIAL REPORT

CRIMINAL INVESTIGATION DEPARTMENT,
SCOTLAND YARD,
12th day of November 1888

SUBJECT: Whitechapel
Murders

Reference to Papers
52983

Duly as reported that an inquest was held this day at Shoreditch Town Hall before Dr. Macdonald, M.P. Coroner on the
body of Marie Jeanette Kelly found murdered at No. 13 Room,
Millers Court, Dorset Street, Spitalfields. A number of witnesses
were called who clearly established the identity of the deceased.
The Coroner remarked that in his opinion it was unnecessary to
adjourn the inquiry and the jury returned a Verdict of "Willfull
Murder against some person or persons unknown."

An important statement has been made by a man named
George Hutchinson which I forward herewith.* I have interrogated him this evening and I am of opinion his statement is true.
He informed me that he had occasionally given the deceased a
few shillings, and that he had known her about 3 years. Also that
he was surprised to see a man so well dressed in her company
which caused him to watch them. He can identify the man and
arrangement was at once made for two officers to accompany him
round the district for a few hours tonight with a view of finding
the man if possible.

Huchinson is at present in no regular employment, and he has
promised to go with an officer tomorrow morning at 11:30 a.m.
to the Shoreditch Mortuary to identify the deceased. Several arrests have been made on suspicion of being connected with the
recent murders but the various persons detained have been able
to satisfactorily account for their movements and were released.

F. G. Abberline, Inspector
T. Arnold, P. Supt.

It seems incredible that George Hutchinson was employed for
just one brief evening to attempt to identify the man he had seen
with Marie Jeanette Kelly. But, obviously, there was no real desire

* This sentence was scored in the margin by either Abberline, or someone
else. Naturally the "important statement" he refers to is no longer contained
in the file.

on the part of either the Home Office or Scotland Yard that the killer should ever be identified.

It is impossible not to recall the Government's attempts to prosecute the seaman James Saddler for the murders. At this point, Salisbury was obviously desperate for a scapegoat and even the worried questions by members of the House of Commons did not sway Home Secretary Matthews from covering up the Crown's intentions to railroad the accused toward a conviction. In every instance, injustice was flaunted as the identity of Jack the Ripper continued to be painstakingly cloaked in mystery.

Before his appointment as head of the C.I.D. in 1903, Sir Melville Macnaghten actually admitted that he had burned the most incriminating papers in the Jack the Ripper File to protect the murderer's family.† At the same time, he compiled a report of his own which pointed at one particular suspect:

> A Mr. M. J. Druit, said to be a doctor & of good family—who disappeared at the time of the Miller's Court murder & whose body (which was said to have been upwards of a month in the water) was found in the Thames on 31st December—or about 7 weeks after that murder. He was sexually insane and from private information I have little doubt but that his own family believed him to be the murderer.

The question that comes to mind is if Macnaghten had burned valuable sections of the Jack the Ripper File in order to protect the murderer's family, why would he then substitute his own equally incriminating report in their place? But if one considers that Macnaghten's report was intended to be read ultimately by others, it seems plausible that, since the Royal Family was in-

† Macnaghten explained his reasons for destroying the file's most incriminating papers to various people at the time (as corroborated by his daughter, Lady Aberconway. Referring to the Jack the Ripper files, Metropolitan policeman Donald Rumbelow writes in his book, *The Complete Jack the Ripper*: "The only recorded destruction of any part of them is attributed to Sir Melville Macnaghten."). It is a matter of record that Macnaghten substituted his own report into the file on February 23, 1894, two years after Eddy's death—although the original of that too has disappeared. All that remains is a revised, typewritten copy whose contents must be regarded as dubious, as Rumbelow eerily points out: "until it is known with any certainty who revised them and why."

volved, this would be a most clever method to throw suspicion off Eddy, diverting it in this case toward a convenient suicide.

Macnaghten in his summary report also states:

No one ever saw the Whitechapel murderer.

This was untrue. In fact, the murderer had been identified on three occasions by three separate witnesses: Police Constable William Smith, prior to the murder of Elizabeth Stride; Joseph Lawende, moments before the slaying of Catherine Eddowes; and George Hutchinson, who followed the murderer and his victim, Marie Jeanette Kelly, back to her room off Miller's Court. All three had been the same man whom they described as young (late twenties to early thirties), about five feet seven or five feet eight inches tall, with a light moustache. It is notable that each time the killer's description was given, it was confused by the police in some way. And in the last instance, it was not even allowed to be presented at the victim's inquest.

Obviously when Macnaghten states that "no one ever saw the Whitechapel murderer," his intention is to add to the mystery, rather than to solve it. But his blatant admission that he burned incriminating papers contained in the file is nothing short of criminal.

Dr. Thomas Stowell's article published in *The Criminologist*, by Nigel Morland, focused for the first time on the true killer. Its impact was felt throughout the world, but it cost Stowell his life.

Unfortunately, the same powers which led Stowell to his death are still at work, in London, poised to overwhelm anyone who investigates too earnestly or stumbles too near the truth.

Epilogue

Perhaps Dr. Stowell's son's burning of his father's dossier of evidence can be understood, though not condoned, by his cryptic explanation to the press: "I have read just sufficient to make certain that there was nothing of importance. The family decided that this was the right thing to do. I am not prepared to discuss my grounds for doing so." Touched by the same degree of fear which must have overcome his father, his answer to my question: "Do you know what was in the file?" could only have been answered by the similar terse falsehood: "I never discussed the file with him."

Certainly there was much more evidence in Dr. Stowell's dossier than the gardener W. Watters' statement that Eddy did not die at Sandringham. I got the feeling from talking to Stowell's son that he had burned a substantial amount of papers. Being the only person who ever met with the man (reporters from the London *Times* tried, as did representatives from other newspapers throughout the world, but all were unsuccessful), and discussed with him the burning of his father's papers, my feeling, of course, cannot be corroborated, but I did experience a challenge in his statement to me that his father was not the only one who knew the Ripper's identity, that "several people now in their nineties know who the killer was." Unfortunately Stowell's son would not elaborate on who these people are.

It is curious that following Sir William Gull's death, Theodore Dyke Acland moved into Gull's house at 74 Brook Street and took over his practice. It is also noteworthy that Dr. Stowell was Theodore Dyke Acland's student at St. Thomas's Hospital and was a close friend of Acland's wife, Lady Caroline, Sir William Gull's daughter. There is no question that in the course of their friendship, Lady Caroline must have shown Stowell her father's notes (Sir William Gull wrote notes to himself constantly, jotting down bits of experience and indulging in the Victorian habit of inventing maxims to follow, such as the one he eventually had lettered on the wall of his study: "Popularity is the admiration of those who are more ignorant than ourselves.").

Dr. Thomas Stowell was the first one in print courageous enough to reveal the murderer's identity, and the guarded version of his article, carefully edited by Nigel Morland for *The Criminologist* in 1970, left no room for misinterpretation that it could be anyone else but Eddy. As Stowell concluded in the article:

> Justice could not have punished "S"*, for at the time of committing the murders he was a lunatic and was not responsible; he could only have been sent to a lunatic asylum. This is precisely what Sir Charles Warren, Sir William Gull, and the young man's family endeavoured to achieve and actually did achieve. Unfortunately he escaped from his first place of confinement after the murder of Eddowes, but let us remember that dangerous lunatics have been known to escape from Broadmoor. In the case of the Ripper, after the murder of Kelly, he was put under private restraint, given such intensive medical care and skilled nursing that he had temporary remissions of his illness and had returned almost to normality . . .

* Nigel Morland confided to me that Dr. Stowell had originally wished to refer to Eddy as "X." In editing the article, Morland opposed the idea, suggesting to Stowell that he use the first initial of a name, *even his own*. Finally this was the choice Stowell made.

I cannot conceive any other humane way of dealing with a sadly afflicted young man and preventing a continuation of the atrocities which he committed entirely irresponsibly. The fact that the women he murdered were whores does not lessen the gravity of the atrocities although they were women of little worth to the community—victims of bad homes, low mentality and their own laziness and the bad social conditions of their poverty-stricken lives and of the gin palaces. It is safe to say that every one of them was infected with one or both of the venereal diseases. The price for the use of their bodies was twopence, and the cost of a bed in a doss-house was fourpence. If they had not this amount after paying for a few glasses of the gin which alone made life bearable, they spent their night, summer and winter, on the seats in the churchyard of Christchurch, Spitalfields.

Jack the Ripper in his letters said he was "down on whores" . . . it also reflected the attitude of the society which had created them . . .

The women Eddy picked for slaughter were socially defenseless. They had descended to the deepest pit of squalor, and all, except for Marie Jeanette Kelly, were well past their prime as prostitutes. Polly Ann Nicholls, Annie Chapman, Elizabeth Stride, Catherine Eddowes, and Marie Jeanette Kelly were similar in at least one respect. They had all been married, were widowed or had left their husbands, and had children either existing with relatives or in orphan asylums. They were alcoholics and had all experienced terrible privation. They inhabited the doss houses of Spitalfields, except when they did not have fourpence for a bed.

Never during any of their inquests was it mentioned that they might have been sexually assaulted. This point was for some reason lost on the Victorians, even though Eddy's intent was obviously sexual. His satisfaction was apparently achieved through the act of mutilation, if in fact he felt any satisfaction at all. Perhaps, like a character in a bad dream, the act of violence froze his feelings, so that he felt nothing.

Colin Wilson expressed his theory, which is a popular one, that Jack the Ripper "was a homosexual sadist with a hatred of women." Wilson, however, was looking at the killer from a different time span. If Eddy had in fact despised women, it would seem logical that he would have picked the most threatening variety available, certainly not helpless prostitutes. However, if we closely view that age when so much was hidden under the guise of social respectability, another possibility surfaces. The women picked were like Eddy himself, desperate and vulnerable. In destroying each of them, by ritualistically cutting them apart, he was in fact sacrificing himself. It was a communion, rather than an act of hatred.

On January 5, 1889, while Eddy was touring India, a journal known as *The Southern Guardian*, printed an article which gazed more deeply than anything which has been published before or since. The paragraph which follows may have seemed ahead of its time. Or perhaps it ventured so near the problem that the Victorians were too embarrassed to look into it. The title of the article was "Murder and Science":

> Suppose we catch the Whitechapel murderer, can we not, before handing him over to the executioner or the authorities at Broadmoor, make a really decent effort to discover his antecedents, and his parentage, to trace back every step of his career, every hereditary instinct, every acquired taste, every moral slip, every mental idiosyncrasy? Surely the time has come for such an effort as this. We are face to face with some mysterious and awful product of modern civilization.

If someone had made a really decent effort to discover Eddy's antecedents, his parentage, to trace back every step of his career, every hereditary instinct, every acquired taste, every moral slip, and every mental idiosyncrasy, his behavior would not have come down to us today as a dark legacy which so many have taken such pains to hide. I, for one, would have given anything to have read Dr. Stowell's dossier of information, and I feel disappointed that I never will.

But there was more involved than Eddy's pathetic existence. There was the fate of a government, the aspirations of a country fast fading as an empire.

Prince Albert, upon whom the title Prince Consort was conferred in 1857, fearing the rising tide of democracy which was appearing all over Europe, had striven to exalt the personal power and influence of the Monarchy, and had once remarked to Queen Victoria's confidential advisor Christian Von Stockmar, "the exaltation of Royalty is possible only through the personal character of the sovereign. When a person enjoys complete confidence, we desire for him more power and influence in the conduct of affairs."

Albert's ambitions were doctrine. He attempted to train his son to survive in a turbulent democratic climate, but the Prince of Wales's personal character was too much for him to cope with.

After Albert's death, Victoria endeavored to perpetuate her husband's desire for an absolute monarchy, doing all in her power to keep his rigid regimen intact, even going so far as to demand that every future heir be named Albert Victor, combining the names of the founders of that dynasty which rules England to this day.

Unexpectedly, the bloody career of Victoria's first namesake (the present Queen's great-uncle), Prince Eddy alias Jack the Ripper, shook the concept of "the exaltation of Royalty" to its foundations. At that point, "the Court," headed by Lord Salisbury, stepped forward to reinforce the station of the Monarchy by ridding it of its greatest threat. In exchange for disposing of Eddy, "the Court" has dictated to the Royal Family ever since.

On December 10, 1936, Edward VIII was forced to abdicate because he wished to marry a divorcée (even though Lord Rothermere, strongly supported by other influential men, proposed that Edward should marry her and remain King, withholding from his wife the title of Queen Consort). To say that Edward VIII was treated shabbily after his abdication is an understatement. His brother, George VI, on orders from "the Court," accorded Edward the title of Royal Highness for himself alone. His wife was excluded from enjoying her husband's rank—a decision which deeply wounded Edward and the legality of which was questioned.

In the 1950s, the cold shadowy hands of Albert, Victoria, and Salisbury once more could be felt when Queen Elizabeth's younger sister, Princess Margaret, announced that she was in love with the divorced Peter Townsend. Within a very short time, this lovely young lady was forced by the phantom powers which still rule England to give him up.

Eddy's shadow still haunts the English, and in the alleys of Whitechapel, which curiously are little changed from the time of the Ripper, one feels his restless spirit. Perhaps this was the reason Eddy's brother, George V, after the death of his mother, wrote to a reader of the *Psychic News,* who had allegedly received a message from Alexandra:

> It is very kind of you to send me such an inspiring message from my dear mother. I fully understand what she has thought fit to convey to me through your instrumentality. My mother is constantly with me watching and guiding my private affairs. I appreciate her message about "a dark cloud shadowing the home but a happy reunion in the land of eternal sunshine."

Bibliography

Following the publication of Dr. Stowell's article in *The Criminologist*, two books written by British authors (*Clarence* by Michael Harrison and *Jack the Ripper* by Daniel Farson) attempted to refute the theory that the Duke of Clarence was Jack the Ripper.

The conclusions in Daniel Farson's *Jack the Ripper* were unfortunately based solely on Sir Melville Macnaghten's notes in the Jack the Ripper File, which Macnaghten himself admitted that he substituted for the authentic records he destroyed to protect the murderer's family. Thus, as I discussed in Chapter 18, Macnaghten became part of the conspiracy to protect the Royal Family by pinning the crimes on Montague John Druitt, a suicide found in the Thames several weeks after the murder of Marie Jeanette Kelly. It is Farson's error that he accepts Macnaghten's fiction as fact, and accuses Druitt of the murders.

Michael Harrison's book, *Clarence*, points the Ripper out as Eddy's lover, James K. Stephen, and extensively documents that he did, in fact, author the letters to the police, including the one which accompanied the kidney of Catherine Eddowes (*see illus-*

tration). He finds a striking similarity between the forming of the letter "K" in the letter to George Lusk and the initial "K" of James's signature. (Much more conclusive, I felt, was the opinion given to me by a curator in the Manuscript Division of the New-York Historical Society who recognized that the most telling similarity to James's signature was the word "whil," ending the second to the last line of the message. He also felt that the writer of the letter, in an attempt to disguise his own handwriting, had changed the angle of the paper in order to form upright letters.) Harrison bases his theory on Dr. Stowell's use of the letter "S" to depict the Ripper (wrongly supposing that on some subconscious level Stowell was suggesting that "S" stood for Stephen). As I have mentioned, as the result of Nigel Morland's suggestion, Stowell used his own first initial.

Fellow British author Donald Rumbelow in his book, *The Complete Jack the Ripper*, most effectively refutes Harrison's theory: "What evidence then is there for Harrison's theory that Stephen was the Ripper? His explorations are elaborate, ingenious and often amusing; but they cannot be taken too seriously. Harrison argues that the inevitable termination of the homosexual relationship which might have existed between the two men aggravated Stephen's jealousy and made him look for ways of revenging himself on Clarence. But why, one asks, should the brutal murder of five unknown East End prostitutes upset the heir to the throne?"

A logical question, when, in reality, one realizes that the reverse was true.

The following sources were essential to the researching of this book. They include pamphlets, newspapers, and periodicals published prior to 1892:

Brewer, John Francis, *The Curse Upon Mitre Square*, A.D. *1530–1888*, 72 pages. London: Simpkin, Marshall, 1888.
British Journal of Photography, page 105. London, February 17, 1888. Article on the use of eyeball photography to identify murderers. November 16, 1888, page 723. Records use of photographs at Kelly murder.
British Medical Journal, "The East End Murders: Detailed Lessons,"

pages 768–69. London, October 6, 1888. Urged that the police "need to be quickened by a higher sense of public morality."

Commonweal, the organ of the Socialist League. London, edited by William Morris, 1888 through 1889, when the anarchists gained control.

Daily News, London. Continuous commentary on the murders and inquests.

Daily Telegraph, London, 1888 to 1892. In the issue of October 4, 1888, propounded that the police had the right to stop pedestrians and search them for knives.

East London Advertiser.

East London Observer.

Evening News, London.

Evening Standard, London.

Fox, Richard Kyle, *The History of the Whitechapel Murders: a Full and Authentic Narrative*, 48 pages. New York: Fox, 1888.

Hansard's Parliamentary Debates, February 17 to March 9, 1891. A record of minutes in the Lower House of Parliament. Questions about treatment of Saddler, who was charged with the murder of Frances Coles.

Hayne, W. J., *Jack the Ripper: or the Crimes of London*, 37 pages, 1889.

Justice, London. Voice of the Social Democrats.

Lancet, London, 1888 through 1889.

Pall Mall Gazette, London. Details murders and inquests and suggests that the police use bloodhounds, beagles, women detectives, and pugilists in drag.

Police Gazette, London, 1888.

Spectator, London, March 7, 1891, pages 335–36. Establishes that Frances Coles was a Ripper victim and points out that the Ripper would have remained equally undetected in Paris, Vienna, or New York.*

The Standard, London.

The Star, London, 1888. In the issue of September 24, George Bernard Shaw put forth the Socialist point of view in his article "Blood Money for Whitechapel."

The Times, London, 1888–89.

Warren, Sir Charles, "Sir Charles Warren Defends the Force," in the *Pall Mall Gazette* and the *Daily News*, London, October 4, 1888.

* Author's note: Most certainly, especially if the Government went to equal lengths to cover up his identity.